STORIES OF GILGAL

A collection of stories, memoirs, and interviews from Gilgal Inc.

Written and Edited by
Catherine Jackson and Naitnaphit Limlamai

Gilgal Inc.
Restoring Homeless Women with Addictions

ABOUT US:
Gilgal is a Christ-centered recovery residence for women who are homeless due to drug and alcohol addiction. Through our one year, two-phase program, we provide food, clothing and housing as well as a full range of addiction services, spiritual nourishment, life skills, and client aftercare. We are located in Atlanta and currently serve the metro area as well as greater Georgia.

Gilgal is 501c3 designation and relies upon generous donations from individuals, churches, businesses, foundations and community organizations. We are a member of the Georgia Association of Recovery Residences (GARR) and accept women without regard to race, nationality, or religious creed.

OUR MISSION:
To educate, equip, and empower women to embrace a future free of drugs/ alcohol by utilizing their fullest potential in a God honoring way through day treatment, counseling, and life skills development.

OUR VISION:
Assist women in breaking the cycle of defeat, that led them to drug and alcohol addiction, by replacing it with a cycle of victorious living through Christ Jesus.

OUR VALUES:

Using the Bible as our guide, we will:

Exercise integrity: doing the right thing at all times
Deliver best service offerings to our clients and employees
Treat clients with dignity and worth
Exercise sound fiscal accountability for individuals and organizations who invest in us.

CONTACT US FOR MORE INFORMATION:

To learn more about how you can help the women of Gilgal who are "Reclaimed Renamed and Forever Changed" visit our website at www.womenofgilgal.org. You can also follow is on Facebook and Twitter.

To connect directly with a Gilgal representative call our office at 404-305-8007 or send an email to info@womenofgilgal.org. CHANGE HAPPENS AT GILGAL and you can be part of it!

In the past several years I have been privileged to meet some of the most amazing and talented women. Women whose lives have been impacted by their choice to use mind altering drugs. They have already lost so much by the time they get to Gilgal...dignity, family, relationships, years of their lives (our average age is 41, most clients started using drugs as teenagers), health, freedom, money, self-worth, jobs. They carry the scars (physically, emotionally, and spiritually) of their former lifestyle - life was not working for them on the other side of Gilgal's entry door. But, they also carry the hope that life can get better. And that is where my Gilgal story begins for each of them.

The women who participate in our programming are homeless as a result of their struggles with drugs and/or alcohol. They are over the age of 18. At least 72 hours away from their last high. Willing to commit to a twelve-month program and they want sobriety.

"...but do you have a "Yes" in your spirit?" Are you willing to give up on your old ways to risk trying something new? Are you willing to do the work on the inside so that a real change occurs or is it just an outside job? And their answer to those questions will set the trajectory for their life as a woman of Gilgal.

We have been so blessed to have a supportive board of directors, a caring staff, and fabulous volunteers that pour in to our women. Prepare to be inspired as you read about the changed lives of women who share about their Gilgal story...

Val Cater
Gilgal, Inc.

When Catherine approached me to work with her on this project, I was honored and thrilled. In working alongside her as author and editor of the stories of the women, graduates, volunteers, and staff of Gilgal, I have been nothing short of amazed at the power of Christ's love in all of our lives. We present to you here the results of His work.

The stories that are enclosed within this volume are snapshots of lives, and are meant to present a glimpse of the lives of all those who come in contact with Gilgal. We hope that we have honored their stories and their histories.

Although we are in awe of the work of Christ, Ms. Val, and her staff, we know that Gilgal does not work for all women. Please refer to the Epilogue for updates of the current clients since the writing of their stories.

Catherine & Naitnaphit
September 2016

Table of Contents

"To tell you my story is to tell of Him."

"My Story" Big Daddy Weave

We dedicate this book to Ms. Val Cater, without whom there would be no Gilgal, and to every client, staff member, and volunteer that has come through Gilgal's doors. Thank you for being willing to share your stories, and by extension, a piece of yourself. This book could not have been written without you.

OUR STORIES

MS. VAL, DIRECTOR

Co-authors Catherine J. and Nait-naphit L. sat down with Ms. Val Cater, founder of Gilgal, to hear her story.

CJ: How did you found Gilgal?

VC: Yes, the founding of Gilgal was not anything I was looking for. As I tell the story, something that was just an out of body experience for me. My husband began investing in 1998 or so and in 2003 or 2004, he bought the property, the house where the women sleep. He came home so excitedly, "Oh Val, this is a different kind of property I bought!" It was a burnt-out crack house, it was in foreclosure, there were people who were active in their addiction living there. And he went and bought this property and said "You oughta think about doing something for women."

And of course, I'm thinking no, I'm not interested in doing that. I had a pretty busy lifestyle at the time, I had two kids, they were 7 and 9 at the time, so busy with all their soccer games and football games and homework and all of those things. I was also part of the Lay counseling ministry at my church, so I was very busy. Oh! And I ran my own business, and I did have a husband at the time [laughing]. So, I was just a tad busy. And so the idea of taking on another thing was not of any interest to me. So, I said no and was done with the matter.

So time passes and a couple weeks later he comes back and goes, "you know, there's something totally different about this property. It's the only house on the street. The neighbor is a church, you know, you do counseling at the church, you should really oughta think about doing something for women." The second time that he asked I'm of course saying in my mind, what does he not understand about no means no? But I decided that God could speak through my husband and I just prayed what I consider a prayer of surrender. "Lord, know You can speak through Tommy, but if You want me to do this I need a neon light. I don't want to jump in this just because Tommy wants me to do it. I need to know from you that it's definitely what you want." You know, I call that my prayer of surrender, but, um, I definitely needed a neon light.

Instantly, people began to appear in my life, just little by little. I said instantly, but, literally, it was little by little people began to appear in my life. One such person was Luc Hall from the Mary Hall Freedom

House. Lucy comes by and she looks at the work my husband's done, looks at the property and the layout, and says "Well, this would be great for a recovery residence, you might want to talk to Diane from the United Way." Couple of days later, Diane calls me, and, you know, in the meantime, I'm thinking, okay, Lord, you may want me to do something. But Diane called me and she comes by and sees what we're doing and looks around. And she says, "You know, this is exactly the kind of thing we like to invest in. We'd like to give you a $300,000 start-up grant." And so I'm thinking that maybe we have a little flickering going on, okay, thank you, Lord. Because that would give us what we needed in order to get started. I could hire

a professional staff, so it's not all dependent on me. I'm a mathematics major, talking about doing human services, so what do I know?

So, that's how we got started. You know, we're a Christ-centered program. I even said to her, "now I want to make sure you know we're Christ-centered." She said, "oh no that's fine, as long as you're not proselytizing." I said, "oh what's proselytizing?" She said, "you know, as long as you don't make them listen to a sermon before they eat." I said, "Well Jesus wouldn't do that! I'm not doing that." You know we present the gospel, but we don't proselytize by their standards.

NL: What line of work were you in before?

VC: Okay, so it's an interesting thing too. I graduated from the University of Alabama (Roll Tide!) with a degree in mathematics. Both my folks were college professors, and they both taught math, you know we did calculus at the kitchen table. I thought everybody was doing algebra equations and trigonometry, you know all these kinds of things, we were solving word problems when I was just a little kid: "Oh! I know the answer!" And that's what my parents did. So, I graduated from the University of Alabama with a major in mathematics and a minor in computer science back in the eighties, and I worked corporate at IBM, worked there for many years. Left IBM, worked at the Paralympic Games, by the time I left IBM, I was on executive loan for the Paralympic Games in '96. All during that time, I became a part of the Lay counseling ministry at my church. So, I do biblical counseling with women and I've been doing that for the past twenty years, and so that's why [my husband] thought, you know, you listen to women, you hear their stories, talk to them about biblical solu-tions, so you should do something for women here.

CJ: So, can you talk about the first year of Gilgal?

VC: Sure, you know, it's an interesting thing you ask that, not a lot of people ask about the first year. And it was really fairly terrifying from the standpoint that, you know, while I had a staff of people around me, what I didn't have was experience as a team. We didn't have any proven, anything that said what we were doing was successful. So here I am, counter to what everyone else is doing in Atlanta, which is an NA/AA model, and I come in with a Christ-centered model. And I just happen to know my God, and I know my God is going to give me better solutions than what the secular world can give me. And that was different. You know I had people tell me, "What you're doing is fine, you just need to take away your Christ centered emphasis." So that was a struggle early on, people telling me to take away the Christ-centered emphasis.

The other struggle was what would we do with women during the day? So, initially, we slept women and sent them out to day treatment. Initially, I had a couple of different places that we would send women out to, so during the day, they would go to outpatient treatment and we would pick them up. We would have a little programming in the evening, and you know, that's what we did. The problem with that is the consistency of message. So, they literally would go to some outpatient places, and they would come back to this Christ-centered environment, and there was a conflict. So, about 2009, we were 4 years into it, we decided that we're going to go and do Transformations@Gilgal. So that was a really big step that we had had programming during the day, that we would take responsibility for what was going on and making sure that a full-rounded curriculum was able to be developed to meet their needs.

CJ: I just want to go back, so, Gilgal, whenever I tell people, this place Gilgal, everyone's like, "Gilgal? What is Gilgal? What is that?" Can you talk about how you came to the name Gilgal?

VC: It's a question I get often. Unlike places where their names are descriptive of what they do, Gilgal has a biblical connotation. You will find the story of Gilgal in the book of Joshua. I love to tell the story, that it was after they had spent 40 years in the wilderness when they cross over to their promised land. One of the first things that they did was camp at this place called Gilgal. And the name in Greek is circle or cycle. It's moving out of a cycle of defeat into a cycle of victory. They were in a cycle of defeat when they were in the wilderness, getting up every morning, marching around, camping, getting manna everyday, what is

that? This is what their life was for forty years, and people are looking at God's chosen people in the wilderness going, "is that the best that God's got for you?" What a defeated life they were living back in those days. They cross over into their promised land and the first thing they did was camp at Gilgal. The men exercised the right of circumcision, there's nothing in the Bible to indicate they had practiced circumcision in the wilderness. As women, we don't circumcise like that, but there's a circumcision of the heart. Very parallel to the women here, there's this crust around my heart, where I was doing drugs, caught in prostitution. God circumcises our heart.

Another parallel is that you know here are God's chosen people and He said when they came to Gilgal, He would roll away the reproach of their Egyptian captivity. The shame that they felt when they were in captivity, He was rolling it away. Same thing for women here, that life that you used to live, God said I will hold it against you no more. As far as the east is from the west, I will remember your sins no more. So that happened at Gilgal.

And the other thing is that they had their Passover, again, there's nothing in the Bible to indicate they celebrated the Passover in the wilderness. The next day, they ate from the fruit of Canaan, you know the big pomegranate, the grapes. Oh, one other thing that was important, when the men were circumcised (and I tell my women this) the Bible tells us they were told to stay at Gilgal until they were healed. Now, that's an easy thing to say to men who have just been circumcised. First off, the grown men were circumcised, and that signified a bunch of things. First off, they had to trust God because they were fighting men. They had to trust that God would protect them while they were healing. He said stay at Gilgal until you are healed, and the Bible tells us one of the first things that happened when they left was they went into battle, Joshua fought the Battle of Jericho. And the same thing happens to my women, they step out the door and they step into battle in the real world. And we just need them to stay here while they're healing so they can be ready for the battles that come in the real world. So that's the significance of Gilgal to me.

NL: That's a great story. When was Gilgal established?

VC: 2005.

NL: So between 1996 and 2005, what happened?

VC: I was, in 1996, I had left IBM, I was working, I had given birth to my first child.

I personally made the decision at that time, while I was working for someone else, here I have this brand new baby, and young lady a little girl. I know I'm going to tell her like my folks told me, you can do anything you want to in life, so I decided I would start doing that as a model for her in my own life. So, I started my own business, and I ran a business where I sold backup in storage systems. Because, you know, I came out of the IT world, so I had sold backup in storage systems to colleges, universities, to places, like the city of Savannah, a lot of big accounts. That's how I put my kids through private school, sustained myself, you know my husband worked, that's how I did a lot of stuff.

NL: So what was the transition between the business world and being the director of Gilgal like?

VC: Well, see, the difference is going from for-profit to nonprofit. I'm very familiar with the for-profit world. I buy low and I sell high, right? And all of the rest of it is mine. That's it, you know you think about it in any business that' what they do. WalMart, same thing, they buy it for as little as possible and sell it for as much as possible. And the rest of it I call profit to my stockholders, and I was always the primary stockholder, all was good [laughs]. When I moved to the nonprofit arena, it was different because none of it is mine. This is a charity with a public trust, and so, when money comes in, instead of knowing it's all mine right away, now I'm going, okay I have to manage every dime and every penny, making sure auditors were a part of it, so that my board knows we're spending money properly and wisely. And also, I don't have a product to sell, my product is the changed lives. So when I write letters to potential contributors, the product is the changed life of a woman at Gilgal. I have to say would you invest in change, in a changed life, would you invest in reconciling families? Would you invest in making this woman a productive member of society? That's what we have here at Gilgal.

NL: One of the big mottos here is "Change happens at Gilgal." What changes have you seen in yourself?

VC: You know, that's an excellent question. I think that my faith has grown deeper. I will tell you I've been a Christian since I was nine years old. I've had to trust God for things to me and my family, but it takes you to a whole other level when you are dealing with someone whose situation is so dire, and you can look at them and say, "You know what, we're going to trust God for this, and we're going to pray about it" and then God shows up and shows out. And that is, you know, I'm never shocked when He does things, but that is always an amazing thing to me. I still get amazed with this front row seat that He gives me and see judges change their heart for women who should be in prison and people see the difference that is made here. That is a big thing that he's allowed me to see where I know that I'm different, my faith has grown deeper, and I guess I just have a bigger faith today than when I first started.

We've been at the moment where we don't have any money, and I've had to look at my staff and go, "oh, I don't know how we're going to pay you," and then someone comes in with a $50,000 check because we're on our knees, Lord, how are we going to do this? You're going to have to help us.

NL: How do you select your staff here?

VC: Well, you know, first I've had to look at what it is we're needing a person to do. So, for an administrative assistant, so of course I want someone with those skills to help me get those things done…

NL: How many people work at Gilgal?

VC: Five, including me. But you know, so taking a look at technically what that job is going to do, but even looking bigger than that, especially those who have daily interaction with the women. For me, it's important that they have a faith that they will be able to talk about with the women because the women that we serve, it's kind of a fragility that goes there. They've been in the world, they've heard the story about this Jesus, but then they've seen Christians behave in manners that were not Christlike, so what's different about your Jesus?

Are you going to be able to love someone when they've cussed you out? Are you going to be able to model what Christ's behavior was? There's that quality that I'm looking for in each staff member. They've got to be able to walk it out. You know, I will say, to my residential staff, and that's Deborah. They have the unique position that they get to live with the women and the women get to see what a Christian looks like when they wake up in the morning. Are you grouchy? Not that I can't have a bad morning before I've had my coffee, but they get a chance to see it. Versus me, they never know whether I'm beating the dog at home, but with Deborah they see it. I need someone who can live it out in a tough moment. Trust me, I have to live it out in tough moments because they also see through that too. Some of the

smartest and brightest women I know are women who have been clients here. Don't be fooled by the fact that they've had addiction because they are very gifted, very talented, and they can spot a fake, so we just have to be authentic with our love for the Lord.

NL: What is your vision for Gilgal?

VC: You know, when we talk about vision, we have this stated vision that says we want to break the cycle of defeat and help women move into the cycle of victory through Christ Jesus. That would be our written vision. But when you talk about my personal vision for Gilgal, I'd like to see us in a position where we're fully funded with a reserve and we actually own this block. That's the thing we're working on. We already own the side of the block we're on. We'd like to own everything that's back behind us and everything other than where the automotive place is. We want to own it and we'd like to be able to tear this building down and build a place where we can serve more women.

That's what I'd like to do, and then from there, what I really want to do is have us in a position where we have permanent housing for women. One of the toughest things that happens in this population, especially those women who've come in that have been using for a long time, maybe they have felonies, this idea of getting an apartment, it's hard to get an apartment if you're a felon. So I'd like to have housing where our women can move into apartments where they can be unified with their kids, still clean and sober living. Still have to take urine tests, still have to commit you're not bringing drugs on property, but I'd like to create a more permanent solution, and from there work with our women so they can become homeowners. On a track where you leave Gilgal, you can keep your job, manage your apartment, and then we can get you to a point where you can be a first-time home buyer. I've had maybe a couple of women in the ten years that I've been doing this, where they're actually now homeowners, which says to me, you know, it works. And I want the women to have that vision, where you know, I can own a home. How many apartment dwellers do I serve that think that's all that I can do, or that I always have to live in substandard housing, and I want them to know better than that. That's what I'd like to see, just as a personal goal. Setting free, letting them know you can come from there and end up over here. Sometimes painting a vision for them because they didn't know it was possible.

CJ: So what's the toughest part about Gilgal?

VC: I think the toughest part is sometimes hearing some of their stories. And to recognize that they didn't really have a chance. We've been so blessed, you know? I've been so blessed. I'm looking at both of you guys, you've been so blessed. It's just some of their lives, the stories that they tell you, I can't even imagine it in my wildest dreams. So that's tough hearing their stories, but then it's also tough trying to paint a vision for them that they can grasp hold of, to know that there's a way out, and sometimes we're successful and sometimes we're not, and that's tough. Because we serve grown women, and they need to make their own decisions, and I'm constantly reminding them, you get to make your own decisions for what's best for you and your family, no one's going to force you into anything. And so honoring their individuality and who they are enough to know they have options.

NL: How do you measure your success?

VC: I don't look at it the way a lot of people look at success. You know I used to say, so there are a couple of different ways to look at it. One is a take a look at a woman who's been here twelve months, so I look at those women who have graduated, twelve months they've been here, they're clean and sober. They have jobs that pay a living wage, they have housing that's affordable, but that's not enough. That just says they graduated our program. Those are the three things that let you know they've graduated from the program: they have a job that pays living wage, they have twelve months of clean time, they're committed to their sobriety, and they have housing that's affordable. But I look at success as a year later, they're still working, they're still clean, and they still have housing, and that's what I call success, that they're still doing it.

And I have some women who are still doing it years later and then some who fall back in. But then, over time, I've come to learn that I have women who are successful that didn't graduate the program, for whatever reason. You just think about what really happens here is that we are creating an environment where women come into a relationship with Jesus Christ, and you may have gotten angry with your roommate and moved, or got into a fight with your roommate and were put out of the program as a result, but you have a relationship with Christ and you still are clean, you still are working, and those things are still true in your life, then I look at that as a success, even though you weren't necessarily a Gilgal graduate.

I have lots of women that didn't graduate the program, but are still doing well, and I look at that as a success, if that makes sense to you. It's not like a lot of other places.

"IT'S JUST SOME OF THEIR LIVES, THE STORIES THAT THEY TELL YOU, I CAN'T EVEN IMAGINE IT IN MY WILDEST DREAMS."

The other thing that's tough for us is we are a twelve-month program. There are lots of programs that are 30-day programs, there are 60 and 90 day programs. Those programs it's easy to say, oh we're successful because ninety percent of our women graduate. Well I don't have any such thing happen. As a matter of fact, I will tend to lose women in my first 30 days. That's my highest rate of dropout because you might come in and in that first 30 days you realize, y'all really don't smoke? Oh they thought they were just saying that on the phone. "I ain't giving up my cigarettes." Or, "you're really reading the Bible, every day?" Despite the fact that we have a script and everybody hears the same script. That way I know it's consistent from woman to woman, and even our staff we try to go back over again when they first get here, just as a reminder, and then it's in that first 30 days that we're more apt to lose women. So, yeah, success is one of those things that is very hard to define and then I know there's this other thing that I look at as far as success is concerned. And that is, is God pleased with the work that I do here? And if He's pleased, then it's been a good day. You know, if He's pleased, if His daughters were treated well, then I'm pleased. Lots of different ways to look at that.

CJ: Before I asked you what the toughest part about Gilgal is, but what's your favorite part?

VC: After all these years, my favorite thing is to see families reunited, and to see parents who come up to me and go, "God bless you, Val Cater. I don't know what y'all doing over there, but that is not the same daughter who came into your program." I mean, that is a blessing. The other really sweet thing is when I've had women get married. That one right there is like, you know they're coming to me homeless and addicted to drugs and then to see them ready to commit their lives to someone, that one right there is like, *really*. I cry

at weddings and so that's also very sweet. And also the women who become mothers again and that's also very sweet time. It's just the normal, sweet little things of life that we just enjoy, I just enjoy it more when I see where their lives have come from. That's just always a blessing.

CJ: Anything else you want to add?

VC: I guess I should add that part of that intake process is that I tell you we're a Christian organization, but also, I want us to represent what some of the best qualities of any agency are. Our women do go through an assessment process. That's part of what the case manager does. Each of them has goals for what they want to accomplish while they're here. And those things would be individual based on where you are. For some women that's going to be getting GED, for some it's going to be family reunification. For all women it's going to be a job, it's going to be sobriety, it's going to be some place that I can have affordable housing, but the rest of the things that I work on will be individualized to what's going on in my life. For some women, I might come in and I might weigh too much, some women want to pick up weight. For some women, I'm a cutter, and I want to stop that, you know, so whatever the issues are that you

have, they're that. For some wom-
en it's to reconcile with my family,
or my mom, or maybe I'm in the
process of grieving and to go
through that. So everybody gets an
individualized treatment program.

The other thing that I would tell
you that I love is that, after women
graduate, I love that they come
back and they bless the other
women by talking with them. They
come back; they volunteer here.
There's a Facebook community
that's vibrant, and women will be a
part of that. And they just encourage each other. There's a sisterhood
that has developed among Gilgal
girls that is a beautiful thing to
witness.

1 August 2016

TAMMY M., CURRENT CLIENT

For thirty-one of Tammy's fifty years, drugs and alcohol defined her life. She was held captive in an up all night, sleep all day lifestyle that was governed by cocaine, pills and alcohol. Among the drugs and alcohol were fights and the streets, creating a life completely absent of structure and security, a life Tammy knew kept her mother awake with worry every night.

The tall, lanky woman, with caramel skin and a skittish personality, began her life of captivity after her high school graduation. She began drinking with her friends at a party, which turned into weed, which turned into cocaine. When she moved back to her hometown of Miami, Tammy didn't stop using, and she found herself on the streets, running wild every night, praying to God every time she did a line that it wouldn't be her last.

After years of using and running through the streets of Miami, Tammy reached a low point that made her realize the highs were not worth the risk anymore. She was riding her bike on the way back from picking up drugs and found herself under a bridge that was completely blanketed with fog, blocking all visibility. "When I made it through, I was thinking how stupid I was that a car that didn't have their headlights on could've run me over," says Tammy. She reveals that her sister had been run over by a car and killed just three years earlier, which is what brought Tammy to the breaking point. "That was it. I could've been killed going to get drugs. I said how stupid I was; my mom just lost a daughter," she says.

And that really was it. Soon after the incident on the bike, Tammy called her oldest brother to pick her up from Miami, so she could break free from her captors. He picked her up Memorial Day weekend and brought Tammy to Georgia with him; however, he was drunk and attacked Tammy, so she asked him to drop her off at the hospital instead. From the hospital, Tammy was released to Cobb Behavioral Crisis Center, where she met the social worker that recommended Gilgal to her, a place that Tammy has come to love. "I love Gilgal, the people, the structure...which I've never had in my fifty years of living," she says. Tammy has also noticed some drastic changes in her behavior: she doesn't desire drugs, fighting, or even cussing anymore. "I've humbled myself; I'm grateful for things I took advantage of," she says.

Tammy's time at Gilgal has not only given Tammy peace, through Jesus and Gilgal itself, but it has given her mother an enormous amount of peace as well. "[My mom] is so grateful that I've gone because she was just waiting for the police to pull up to the door and say Tammy's dead...I spoke to her yesterday; she said she can sleep now," says Tammy. Her voice breaks and tears fill her eyes, "She said when she saw the white City of Miami police car, she was going to say, 'thank you, I know,' and close the door." Tammy now gets to talk to her mom on a regular basis because of her phone privileges at Gilgal.

When she graduates Gilgal, Tammy wants to continue her life of clean living, "No drugs," she says. "I don't desire it at all." She also hopes to get a job at a retail store, where she will have the opportunity to move up the ladder and wants to be able to visit her sons, who now live in North Carolina.

As she reflects on the time she's spent at Gilgal, Tammy wants people to know that if you want it, you can find it at Gilgal. She had been learning how to grow closer to Jesus with each day that passes. "This place has helped me grow closer to Him," she says. "I just love Him."

18 July 2016

AISHA F., VOLUNTEER

I was simply looking for a chance to volunteer and give back; never did I think my giving back would impact me as much as it has.

I am one of the newer volunteers at Gilgal Inc. -- I teach the women goal-setting and action-planning strategies, interpersonal skills, and conflict management. My time with the ladies and staff has been a little shy of one year; however, in this short period of time, I have been privy to watching women enter the program as despondent, broken, lost, and rejected individuals whose lives were seemingly irreparable. Society had either given up on them or viewed Gilgal Inc. as the last opportunity for them to "get it right." Just as often as I watched them enter the home in this state of "brokenness," though, I have been privileged to see "change happen!" The change I have seen in the women who courageously and committedly endure the structure and curriculum at Gilgal House is nothing short of remarkable.

Hearing the ladies articulate their commitment to their sobriety and their growing relationship with Christ, watching the women discover and re-discover Christ's love, the hidden treasures that reside within them, and their worth and value has tugged on my heart in ways that I never knew were possible. Seeing the transformation and significant personal growth in the ladies, hearing them say, "Thank you; I enjoy your class and it is really helping me to be better," makes me proud. I am able to say that I helped to sprinkle a little water on the seeds that are planted by Gilgal by enforcing the life skills and spiritual and personal development messages that are communicated daily. Watching the seeds take root and bloom into the flowers -- women -- that God created them to be is absolutely amazing.

But the change isn't just in their hearts, it's in mine too. Because of the commitment of the staff and volunteers at Gilgal House, the tagline of *"Where Change Happens"* couldn't be more accurate. My witness to the change in the ladies has increased my level of commitment towards volunteering and helping those who need assistance in getting back on the right path in life. I initially approached this volunteer opportunity thinking that I would be pouring into the lives of women. The truth of the matter is that the women I have encountered at Gilgal have equally poured into me. Never before had I been interested in nonprofit work or establishing a nonprofit organization of my own. But as a result of the relationships I've made with the staff and ladies of Gilgal Inc., my compassion for the under-served, disenfranchised, and marginalized has now forced me to begin thinking of starting a nonprofit organization to assist women, recently released from incarceration, to secure affordable housing and develop the soft skills needed for employability and marketability. My level of compassion and commitment towards helping and building up others has been inspired by the work of Gilgal.

2 July 2016

DEBORAH M., GRADUATE

I would like to share with you a story of a former Gilgal client who struggled with addiction and in the process lost her marriage, a home, several jobs, self-control and self-respect.

I was an Army brat: my father was in the Army and my family traveled and moved often.

Our family finally settled in my father's hometown of Montgomery, Alabama. I enjoyed living near my grandparents, aunts, and uncles. That was a wonderful time in my life.

Three years later, life as I knew it would change. My father was transferred to Atlanta, Georgia, and the rest of the family soon followed. Once we got settled in Atlanta, my parents decided to divorce.

This was devastating for all of the children, but I took it the hardest. Being the oldest of three, I took on a lot of responsibility at a young age. While my mother worked two jobs, I became the sole keeper of my sister and brother. But I was sad. I missed my Dad and began to resent my mother. All my friends had their mother and father living in the same house and I felt like an outsider around them.

My mother struggled to pay the bills and to keep us fed. Many times I went without food or proper clothing, but my mother refused to ask anyone for help. As I grew older and became self-sufficient, I started making the wrong kinds of friends. I wanted and needed to fit in and this is when I started to experiment with drugs. Marijuana was first and then alcohol, then on to cocaine. I learned to keep secrets, lie, steal, and never ask anyone for help. By the time I was 27 years old, I was hooked. Over the next 20 years, as my addiction progressed, I lost several jobs, family relationships, and was in and out of rehab five times.

One Saturday in October 2009, I woke up after a night binging on drugs and said that I couldn't do this anymore, that this is not for me. I needed to get to a phone. On October 24, 2009, I entered into Gilgal. Before I walked in the door, I stopped and said, "Lord I don't know how this is going to work, but I am willing to try one more time."

Gilgal offered many classes such as relapse prevention, job

readiness, and most importantly Bible studies. I particularly enjoyed a class called "Be Transformed." This is a class that taught how to transform our minds and challenge our belief systems. One of the main lessons that stood out to me was a comparison between the heavenly Father and the earthly father. I believed that both God and my birth father were very similar in that they were both distant and never there when I needed them. After taking several classes, I began to realize my belief system was false.

With this new knowledge, I started to develop a new relationship with Christ. I learned that my drug use was a symptom of deeper issues that I had been struggling with all of my life. I then realized that I do not know how I lived without Christ in my life. In October 2010, I graduated from Gilgal and began my new life. I have been clean and sober for almost six years. I am now a residential manager for Gilgal Inc.

I can truly say that my life was transformed and I thank God for saving me. I never believed that I would have Christ in my life. I also did not think it was possible to live a life clean and sober until Christ showed me a new way of living.

19 July 2016

CHARLOTTE T., VOLUNTEER

The first time I visited Gilgal I realized, "These are my people!" I think I felt at home because it's a place where facades have been removed to reveal the true beauty of humility, simplicity, and hope. It's a place that encourages those who visit to do the same. I've met some courageous women with amazing stories that I hope will remain in my life for years to come.

At Women of Gilgal the slogan is, "Change happens at Gilgal." But it's not just a slogan, and it doesn't just apply to those coming for help. To work there, visit, or volunteer is to experience being changed. There's a basis for this change, the only One who can truly change lives, set us free, and cleanse us from sin is kept center stage: Jesus. So those of us blessed with an opportunity to share in the Gilgal story don't go away unchanged.

I've had the joy of bringing a couple of retreats to the women. We come in to share meals, the Word of God, get alone with God in His Word, and come together to discuss what we're hearing from Him. I remember one time I was driving toward Gilgal for a retreat, ruminating on trusting Jesus to do the work. He is the true Vine; we are the branches. I didn't realize until I got there that I was missing the cord to run the projector which was an important part of the presentation. But trusting the Lord to do the work, we were still blessed and changed by what He showed us and taught us. He has a plan for Gilgal, and it is exciting to watch it unfold.

I'm so thankful I found Women of Gilgal. I came in initially because our Women's Ministry at church had given us some ideas for outreach in our Bible Studies. I don't like to force those things, but Women of Gilgal was one we decided to see if we could bless. As it turned out, Barbara Jackson, who is now on the board of Gilgal, was in the class! That connection made, I met the women, Val, and the staff. Val and I learned we share the same alma mater, and have felt like sisters in many ways ever since. No one networks like the Lord. I continue to rejoice at every opportunity to be a part of what's going on at Gilgal. Not all change is welcome, but the change happening at Gilgal is priceless.

2 August 2016

ROSIE L., VOLUNTEER

I am Rosanne "Rosie" L., a grateful child of God. His plan to continue my transformation into His image led me to a more in-depth study of His word about five years ago. I began a series of Bible studies called Disciple. It was during the first year of this series that I met a young lady who had volunteered at Gilgal and shared her experience there. She and a few of her friends were walking with the Gilgal ladies and preparing them to participate in 5K events. I felt moved by the Holy Spirit to learn more about Gilgal and asked her how I could possibly volunteer there also. She suggested that I go to the Gilgal website and mentioned a video that I should view. After watching the video, I felt more drawn to the Gilgal mission as I have dealt with the issue of addiction in my family as well and wanted to help others facing that challenge.

I filled out the volunteer application online and on it, in response to one of the questions, mentioned my background of teaching line dance classes. My intention was to volunteer to walk with the ladies as the lady in my bible study was doing, but the email that I received from Val requested that I teach a line dance class to the ladies. I accepted her offer and began teaching the weekly class soon after. The love that I have experienced working at Gilgal and the awe that has been evoked by watching the ladies face the challenge of recovery from addiction has enriched my life and kept me coming back for more.

My church, Mt. Zion Methodist, is actually nearby the Gilgal campus. Not long after I had volunteered there, we organized a Missions Event at my church and I suggested that we invite Val to come and give a talk about the mission and work being done at Gilgal. She was happy to do so and as a result, others at Mt Zion have become involved at Gilgal also. We have come to cherish the occasional visits that the ladies make to our Sunday morning church service. I am incredibly grateful that God led me to Gilgal and that now I feel like a part of the Gilgal family. Love, after all, is what makes a family and it is at the root of the connection I have been blessed with there.

26 September 2016

KRISTI Q., CURRENT CLIENT

When trouble comes, where do you turn? For Kristi Q., a small, spritely, green-eyed woman who talked so fast it was hard to keep up with her, it was to do whatever would help her avoid things, to run, and often to run to one of her many addictions: drugs, work, an eating disorder. In fact, about 35 days into her stay at Gilgal, Kristi realized she was "feeling emotions" she "didn't want to feel;" God was revealing things to her as part of her recovery, and she didn't want any part of it. She had a two-year plan to leave Gilgal and try to make it on her own, to take her 19-year-old daughter, flee to Tennessee, lay low, and find work. She says, she "wouldn't have cared what the consequences were. I would have figured it out later."

That was on a Friday afternoon when Kristi developed her plan to leave Gilgal, so she called her probation officer to tell him. But he was out of town. This would give Kristi much-needed time over the weekend to think about what she was going to do.

Unbeknownst to Kristi, she needed someone to talk to about her decision to pick up and run, and there was Ms. Cheryl, a staff member, working late in the office to wait out the Friday traffic. After their conversation and after attending Pastor Turner's church on Sunday, she ended up staying. She realized that "this is where [she] need[s] to be...to have the safety of people to talk to, to be safe and to feel safe. It gets easier as you're here," she says.

Kristi was an upper middle class drug user who had been able to use and maintain her life: a car, a house, a job. But after being arrested and jailed for the first time for violation of her probation for shoplifting, a cellmate, who had been at Gilgal, had started to minister to her. "She never forgot anything she learned here," Kristi says. "She prayed with me every day, did Proverbs with me every day," just like they do in daily Bible study at Gilgal. Kristi had never been in such despair or so scared in her life, but her cellmate "was my angel in jail," Kristi says. "I wouldn't have gotten through it without her. God brought her to me."

Her supportive family called every day to get her into the program. It is hard to be away from 19-year-old her daughter, with whom she is close, but her parents are relieved and grateful because she is in a safe

space, and they want her to get better.

When it comes to Gilgal, even though at first she had a hard time staying, she wants to be here now. "God is in everything here. People say things that I need to hear. The Holy Spirit works through these people," she says. The Holy Spirit gives her the ability to do things that she cannot do on her own, like bring people into her life to convince her to stay when all she wants to do is run.

People love her here. "I've never been in a place where people love you like over here," she says. She's grateful to be here. She knows that "God is here. God has been in my life," she says. "God has brought me up for a reason." Reading the Bible "gets my mind on true things," she says. It's not easy every day, she says, but it could be a lot worse.

Kristi speaks highly of Gilgal, has never seen anything like it, and is glad that she was able to be led here. She doesn't think enough people know about it, though. After graduation, she wants to have a "really good job." She "has a lot of plans" and wants "to come back to Gilgal and give back." She's looking forward to having "enough money to rent a house," where she and her daughter can "move back in there and stay sober, whether it be from drugs or work or an eating disorder." She wants to "find a good home church, a good home group with Christ-like people." She believes that that's the only way she can maintain her new life. "God is the most important part of that picture," she says.

19 July 2016

ROSEMARIE L., VOLUNTEER

"Rosemarie, do you love Me? Feed my sheep!" The question and answer resounded rather quietly, but with firm impact to my spirit at the closure of a Tres Dias Christ weekend experience in the mid 90's. I had no idea at the time that impact would lead to a deeply meaningful fulfillment in ministering to "His sheep" at Gilgal.

Little did I know that the Lord's heartbeat piqued in me in 2012 through Isaiah 61:1-3: "The Spirit of the Lord God is upon me, because the Lord has anointed me, to preach good tidings to the poor; He has sent me to heal the brokenhearted, to proclaim liberty to the captives, and the opening of the prison to those who are bound; to proclaim the acceptable year of the Lord, and the day of vengeance of our God; to comfort all who mourn, to console those who mourn in Zion, to give them beauty for ashes, the oil of joy for mourning, the garment of praise for the spirit of heaviness; that they may be called trees of righteousness, the planting of the Lord, that He may be glorified." Never could I have known that these verses would be as profoundly significant in my journey in Christ towards Gilgal as they became.

Looking back to 1990: the Lord first had to prepare me to be His vessel, so I would be ready to minister to the hurting women He would eventually call to Gilgal. This preparation occurred through Exchanged Life counseling for my own deeply brokenhearted need for His Redemptive Hope, proclaimed in the aforementioned Isaiah passage. So, His stirring increased. I then received Lay counselor training and certification at First Baptist Church Atlanta in 1996, co-laboring with the Lord surely by His Grace, and where I also served with Ms. Val Cater.

Around 2005, Ms. Val obeyed God's call for her to start Gilgal; I was in awe of her obedience, while I was uttering within, "Lord, Gilgal?.. Not me…impossible….I'm unable!" So, I continued my work at First Baptist, but I couldn't ignore His call for long. In 2012, during a heart-riveting Bible Study Fellowship of Isaiah, my Father's voice could not be stilled as Isaiah 61:1-3 pulsed deeply within me and called me intently with His throbbing promise, "...a bent reed I will not break, a smoldering wick I will not extinguish…!" I soon responded, "Yes, Lord, send me to feed Your sheep," and offered to minister the comforting Truth to the women of Gilgal, so they too could hear the freedom from the same bondage and sorrow that had plagued me.

Our Heavenly Father alone defines us -- no upbringing, no resulting lifestyle, no circumstance -- The Lord alone! He permits and even blesses me beyond measure to minister to the courageous women of Gilgal who also choose to say, "Yes, Lord, here I am!"

14 August 2016

MISS SUE., GRADUATE

In 2010, Miss Sue, a revered woman in her mid-sixties, was in a low place. She had lost her father, was in an addictive relationship with alcohol, and was in the hospital for stomach ulcers. It was during her stay in the hospital that Miss Sue's doctor told her it was time for her to seek a long-term rehabilitation program. Because she was financially unstable, Miss Sue's options were limited. "I had to find somewhere, so I called Lawrenceville, they put me in touch with Ms. Val, and I came to Gilgal," she says in her gentle, southern drawl.

When she arrived, Miss Sue found familiarity in the Christian atmosphere of Gilgal. "I grew up in a church. My mother was always taking me to church. She was a good Christian woman," she says. Her childhood was good. She was an only child and was spoiled by her parents. Her father suffered from alcoholism, but there was never any violence or fighting in the house.

Although Miss Sue's childhood was good, it was also very controlled. "We didn't talk about problems," she says. "My mother thought if you avoided them, they would go away." As a result, Miss Sue learned how to hide her true feelings, a practice that plagued her both before and during her time at Gilgal. She was afraid to share her true feelings and began to tailor what she would share to what she thought people wanted to hear. "I was afraid of people judging me," she says.

After ten months at Gilgal, Ms. Val approached Miss Sue and told her she thought Miss Sue was ready to graduate. Still bound by her habit of suppression, Miss Sue agreed with Ms. Val's suggestion, even though she knew she wasn't ready to leave the program. So, she graduated, found a job, and began working long hours.

Exhaustion is a trigger for Miss Sue, and soon after she had left Gilgal, Miss Sue found herself hankering for a taste of alcohol. "I tried to follow the Holy Spirit's guidance," she says, "but sometimes I get weak, especially when I'm tired." She began to think about drinking again. And again, she was silent about her feelings. Miss Sue wanted to be the woman that the members of Gilgal had bragged about at graduation, and that woman was a strong woman. In her desperation to be strong and to resist

36

defeat, Miss Sue relapsed.

When she relapsed, Miss Sue's relationship with God also grew weaker. Exhaustion had not only pushed her to drink, but it had pulled her away from spending time with God. She had fallen away from her dedicated Bible readings and her prayer time. When she got home from work, drained from her day, it was easier for her to let the weariness consume her than it was for her to make the effort to spend time with the Lord. Despite this, Miss Sue was aware that God was still by her side, and she began to take the steps to bring herself back to Him. As a result, she sought out another Christ-centered recovery program. Even though she was seeking help and grounded in her faith, Miss Sue was still tempted by alcohol. "I had this obsession in my mind that I would actually be able to drink alcohol like normal people," she says. For Miss Sue, alcohol gave her a feeling of importance, and more significantly, she thought it allowed her to express herself.

So one afternoon, about two years ago, after finishing her shift at work, Miss Sue gave in and purchased a drink. A drink that almost cost Miss Sue her life. This relapse caused Miss Sue to become very sick to the point where she had to be admitted to the hospital. "I still don't feel exactly right after that relapse," she says. That relapse is a part of Miss Sue now; it reminds her of her old drinking habits. After her near-death experience, Miss Sue knew she had to get help again, so she picked up the phone and begged Ms. Val to let her come back.

This time at Gilgal was much different from her first time. It was filled with honesty and openness, not lying and concealing. She didn't allow herself to stay silent and always shared when she had the opportunity. "When you speak words out they lose their power," she says, "so I wouldn't let a class go by without sharing." About a year later, with her newfound voice, Miss Sue graduated from Gilgal for the second time. She now works in retail and continues to praise God for the many blessings he has given her, both with work and with Gilgal. "Gilgal is the most wonderful thing that's ever happened to me," she says.

19 July 2016

DENISE N., VOLUNTEER

Alice stumbled into a rabbit hole and crash landed in Wonderland; I can relate -- I fell in somewhat the same style and landed in Gilgal. It was a little gentler, but unexpected, and a total game changer.

It was a simple outing. Going with our small church group to share dinner with some women at a rehab center -- to encourage, come alongside for a friendly evening. About 10 of us arrived with cleaning supplies, which we'd been told would be appreciated, and components for a sloppy joe smorgasbord that we combined and ate together. With mutual enjoyment over comfort food, we shared stories, love for Jesus, had a tour, and our group went home.

But, not all of me came home. I suspect that God pinched off a teensy bit of my heart and buried it there while the rest of me climbed into the car and onto I-75 without another thought. At first. But then the little missing bit started tugging. I kept thinking about Gilgal. What might they need? Could I help? What do I even have to offer? The major part of me was wrestling over this mental intrusion. "You don't know these people; they don't know you." "You can't do anything that anybody would need anyway." "You're busy enough already." "Get your mind off this distraction."

The back and forth became so annoying that I figured I'd take the next micro-step and place a tentative inquiry. There's only one area in my life where formal training and passion come together that might be of any value to a Christ centered organization: I have taught the Bible, but so have a million other people. Just in case my uneasiness was a God thing instead of indigestion, I figured that this tiny nod to a step of obedience would satisfy personal leanings and God would probably ascertain that He had better options for Gilgal anyway and we'd be finished with it.

Don't underestimate God's sense of humor. He unrelentingly latches onto the slightest willing individual and moves them down far different paths (or rabbit holes!) than they might foresee themselves. He "chooses the foolish to confound the wise," which I take to mean that He surprises us in His choices. Not Wonderland with Alice, but a wonderful land indeed. I've now been teaching the Bible at Gilgal for several years. Tim Keller uses these words: "By itself, 'heaven' can be an abstract and unappetizing idea. But if you come to taste 'access' with God and realize how intoxicating it is just to have a couple of drops of his presence on your tongue, you will desire to drink from the fountainhead." At Gilgal I find myself in a position to encourage drinking often from God's fountainhead. It's an addiction we can all indulge.

One of my favorite aspects of Gilgal is that it's a delightful captive audience! These women are captivating people who've found themselves at rock bottom, usually open to tasting a new thing, and we learn together. God meets us. There is healing, learning, rejoicing, and He is honored. Nothing is sweeter in this life than to participate in the process of some-body's falling headlong in love with Jesus Christ—out of darkness into light, out of bondage into freedom, out of dismal futility into fruitfulness and abundant life. I am privileged, thrilled, challenged, fulfilled to have a front row seat to observe the transformation that happens at Gilgal; I've come to love each woman I've met at Gilgal—a rich ongoing blessing. As St. Paul says so well, "The one who calls you is faithful and he will do it." He certainly does!

31 July 2016

MAGEN G., CURRENT CLIENT

Magen G. smiles easily. Her hair is pulled into a ponytail to keep it off her face, and she begins her story in her soft voice.

When she was 13 years old, she started doing drugs. Eventually she was hooked on cocaine, living in a poor community in Birmingham with her abusive boyfriend. They were both active in drugs and fighting every day. At one point, she suffered from a broken nose, broken eye socket, and broken finger. While her boyfriend worked, Magen was prostituting. Most of the time he served as her bodyguard. This went on for about 10 months before Magen had enough.

"It's a funny story," Magen begins. On a Saturday, she was almost murdered by three people. By Sunday she had made a call for help, had moved out of the place she and her boyfriend shared, and ended up at the hospital. Another woman who had stayed at Gilgal recommended it for Magen. "I was in the right place at the right time," Magen says.

When she arrived she had a hard time with the other women. "On the streets," she says, "I wasn't allowed to have friends. I avoided other women." Yet she knows Gilgal is where she belongs. Right away she could feel Ms. Val's love. "She always lets me know that she cares about me," Magen recounts. "I don't get that from anyone else in my life right now. When someone you don't even know looks you in the face and tells you they love you -- she's very caring and very loving and let's me know I'm loved."

This love has helped Magen stay sober for more than 40 days. She's "thawed out from the drugs" and is ready for the many motivations to stay at Gilgal and pursue Christ. She now recognizes that "God is desperately screaming for me to come to Him," she says. There are "behaviors I'd love to change," and through the work of the Holy Spirit she knows she can accomplish them. At Gilgal she has reconfirmed her relationship with Christ and is getting to know Him on a personal level. And although sometimes she gets antsy, she keeps hearing the words "be still" and she knows that this is the place she's supposed to be. She says, "If yo feel like you cannot stop using drugs or are in a terrible relationship, this the place to be. If you don't know Christ and you want to know him, you

need to be here."

She's not ready yet to be "out there on [her] own," but one day she knows she will be. Her family is very proud that she "had the courage to leave everything behind." She's looking forward to spending time with her grandson and is open to God's plan for what He wants of her next. "God wants to change everything around," she says.

18 July 2016

JILL W., VOLUNTEER

My first introduction to Gilgal was in the summer of 2015 when my friend, Charlotte T., with the Abide in Him ministry held a retreat at Gilgal, and I offered to help with it. All I can say is that during the hours spent at Gilgal for the retreat, I knew I had to come back. I can't even really explain it except to say that I had a deep love for these women that was so strong — I knew it had to be from the Lord. I had no idea how God would use me at Gilgal, but there was no doubt in my mind that He did want me to join the Gilgal team.

You see, for about two years, the Lord had been teaching me a recurring lesson — to break every yoke in my own life -- anything and everything that was keeping me from loving the LORD with all my heart, mind, soul, and strength. Isaiah 58 came up over and over again. I knew the Lord not only wanted me to hear it, but He wanted me to act in faith, tearing down my strongholds. And you know what? Strongholds are really hard to break, but God is stronger! He gives us His Spirit and He gives us one another to be a part of the journey together!

I love the openness and honesty at Gilgal, I love the sisterhood there, I love their approach to getting to the root of the chains, and I love their commitment to hear and obey the LORD fully. We, Americans, are doing a really good job these days of "pretending obedience to God." But Psalm 81:15 says, "Those who hate the LORD would *pretend* obedience t Him." I have never been very good at pretending to be someone I'm not, but personally I want to be done with any and all kinds of "pretending" obedience to Him; I want to obey Him fully!

Obedience to the Lord is real at Gilgal. We pray together, we read God's Word together, we learn together, we cry together, we encourage one another, we share our hearts with one another, and we trust God individually and collectively!

For me, it's not about volunteering at Gilgal because I feel sorry for the women struggling to overcome addictions; as a matter of fact, I have great respect for them for facing their addictions head on with the One, the ONLY ONE, who conquers all sin and addictions. I volunteer at Gilgal because I recognize I have my own addictions and fleshly tendencies that the Lord wants to break me of as well. We all need each other! The exciting part is that we serve an amazing God who constantly blows our minds because He is changing our hearts as we yield ourselves to Him and to His Word. It's a glorious thing to see transformation take place from the inside out!

Gilgal is a God-fearing, God-honoring, Spirit-led organization where change happens. This change is possible because we serve a risen Savior who died to sin and rose again so that not only do we have hope for the future, we have hope for today — to no longer be slaves to sin, but to truly be free in Christ. The Lord continues to work on me, and in this process, it is such a joy to share what He is teaching me and to learn from the women of Gilgal what God is teaching them. I truly love the Gilgal women, they are my forever sisters in Christ and it is an honor to be in this amazing journey of life with them!

16 August 2016

SHELLY F., CURRENT CLIENT

"I'm the person that nobody expected to stay," says Shelly in a thick Bronx accent. Her black hair is pulled into a disheveled up-do, and her demeanor suggests a straightforwardness that northerners are famous for. Shelly, a three-time convicted felon and a drug user, has been revolving in and out of prison's doors since 2006. It was where she had her daughter in 2006 and where she learned to beat the penal system. When she was arrested at Lenox Mall for credit card swiping, while on one of her stealing sprees, Shelly knew she had to be done with prison. "I knew [prison] was not going to make a difference to me," she says. "I needed another alternative." That alternative turned out to be Gilgal. Like many other women at Gilgal, Shelly is court-mandated and is not allowed to leave Gilgal until her graduation date, which, after a long year of unexpected trials, is just three weeks away.

When the tough girl from the Bronx first arrived at Gilgal, she had no intention of staying: "as soon as they dropped me off, I [was] going to leave," she says. Circumstances, however, never gave her the opportunity to desert the place offering her a second chance.

Just as she was settling into Gilgal's routine, a 2012 warrant resurfaced. She had violated the terms of her probation with 19 felonies in another Georgia county. After much resistance and encouragement from Ms. Val and Ms. Cheryl, Shelly turned herself in, something she had never done before. When Shelly showed up in court, her probation officer was stunned, and immediately noticed there was something different about the girl who had always evaded doing the right thing. "[They] didn't think I was going to come," says Shelly. She knew this change could only be attributed to Shelly's time at Gilgal.

Before she was rearrested and had even "phased up," Shelly had found her first legal job at a local store, had spoken to the students at Martin Luther King Jr. High School, and had been sober for several months. A clear contrast to the woman she had been just months before. Despite this obvious change, Shelly was detained in South Georgia for longer than she had hoped, and she began to doubt that God had plans to bring her back to Atlanta. When she finally got a court date, the judge wasn't convinced of Shelly's transformations, but upon hearing Ms. Cheryl's testimony of

Shelly's progress, he allowed Shelly to come back to Gilgal, where God has continued to prove His faithfulness.

When she got back to Gilgal, Shelly received both better hours and better pay at her job and was finally given the opportunity to visit her daughter, whom she had not seen for four years. Now, even when she's tempted, Shelly couldn't imagine leaving Gilgal. "I just want to change my life and do the right thing," she says.

While at Gilgal, Shelly has also established a relationship with God. She had been to church before, but it was never for the right reasons. "I would go to church to smuggle stuff," she says. Now, Shelly can see God working in her life in every situation. She's experienced His deep love through the current residents, as well as the volunteers and staff members. "I look at Ms. Deborah like a mother," she says. "The love that you're shown here – I don't think there's another rehab that's anything like this."

During her time at Gilgal, Shelly's family has always been there for her. "I have a very, very supportive family," she says. "I was just so deep into my addiction and sin that I didn't realize how good I had it." They, too, have noticed the miraculous changes Shelly has undergone during her months here: "when I went home for the first time, my family was like, who are you?"

Between her growth and her changes, however, Shelly has faced many hardships this past year. In addition to her probation violation, Shelly has seen some of her closest friends walk out of Gilgal's doors, her community service records have gotten lost, and a few months ago, she was hit by a car while crossing the street. "The devil works," she says. "He is never tired of bothering you." The Shelly from a year ago would have let it get to her, but now she takes everything as it comes and trusts that it's in God's timing. "If you allow this program to help you, it makes you become very humble; I would've been flipping earlier today," she says, laughing.

Suddenly, the boisterous woman pauses for a brief moment. The intensity in her voice has faded and has been replaced with slow, thoughtful speech. "I'm to the point where it's kind of like a bittersweet thing," she says. "I want to leave, but I don't…You meet so many good people here…they don't even know you from nowhere, and they are just so loving and caring." Shelly is grateful for all the staff and volunteers, those she knows and those she's never met before, for all that they've done for her and the other women, and for the home they've created for her. "You know, for some people that've never gotten to experience what love really is, if you don't figure it out here, I don't think you're ever going to figure it out," she says. "Getting to know Jesus, this whole place, it all revolves around one thing."

Recently, Shelly paid a visit to the District Attorney's office to say thank you for giving her the second chance that changed her life. "I wasn't tired; I wasn't tired of prison," she says. "I had everything I ever wanted…I was comfortable and didn't have any responsibility." Now, she has that responsibility, with her job and her daughter, and she cherishes it. As her graduation date approaches, Shelly admits that she is sad to leave, but knows "[she] has to do what is right for [her] daughter," she says. She's looking forward to watching her daughter graduate from the third grade without having to worry about who will recognize her from the news.

"I'm just thankful I'm still alive," she says. Without Gilgal, Shelly isn't sure where she would've been after prison, but now she has a future to look forward to. She wants to give back to the community and speak to women in prison, and after graduation, she hopes to get the probation papers that will allow her to go back home to her family in New York. "I feel like God brought me this far, He can move a piece of paper," she says. "I it's really meant for me to go, then I'll go. If it's not, then He has another plan for me. I'm just content, you know?"

19 July 2016

PIONEER DRIVE CHURCH, VOLUNTEERS

RICK C: ADULT SPONSOR

My name is Rick C., and I am one of the adult sponsors for the Pioneer Drive Baptist Church High School Choir in Abilene, Texas. It was my great honor to travel with our music minister, Danny B., from January 31-February 3, 2016 to Atlanta to make preparations for our summer choir tour/mission trip. On Monday, February 1, 2016, Danny and I met with Matthew S., the associate music minister and youth minister at First Baptist Church in Atlanta. In our meeting with Matthew he had prepared a list of possible mission work locations for our group to serve with when we came back June 18-25. I remember like it was yesterday, the first person he put us on the phone with was a lady he called Ms. Val. Of course Ms. Val is Val Cater, the founder and director of Gilgal. In our phone conversation you could just feel the passion in Val for the women she gets to minister to each day. We asked her if Danny and I could come by to visit with her about our upcoming trip, and she immediately said yes. So, Danny and I made arrangements to come over to see the facilities at Gilgal and to sit down with Ms. Val.

When we arrived, Val had one of her ladies to give us a tour of the facilities, then we sat down in Val's office. Wow! What an amazing lady Val Cater is! She began by sharing how she came to open Gilgal and then asked us about our group and we discussed some of the projects we might do with our group when we came back in June. One of the things Val showed us in her office was the inch of paint, or should I say lack of paint, around the ceiling. Another group that had come to paint her office had run out of time before they could paint where their tape had been. Val expressed to us that that inch served as a reminder to her that sometimes groups can't get everything done that they plan on doing and not to expect too much. It was at that moment I made the promise to myself that one of the things we were going to do when we came was to paint her office, all of her office! When Danny and I went to the car to leave I told him that I wanted us to paint Val's office for one of our projects. I shared this story with our choir several times when we returned from the Preview Trip to Atlanta. Val expressed that she always wanted to have more projects than a group like ours could get done so that there never came a time when everyone was standing around with nothing to do. Through our conversations over the next few months before going back to Atlanta Val and I had discussed these projects. When we arrived at Gilgal on June 22 to begin work, I believe we had 30 projects. I can proudly say that we got 29 of those projects done in our 4 days of serving at Gilgal.

The thing is, the projects are not the story of what our group experienced at Gilgal. The story came with meeting and serving alongside of the ladies at Gilgal. When we met on that Tuesday morning, the first thing we did was to have praise and worship time, then Val shared with our group about how she was led by the Lord to begin Gilgal. Val also had one of her ladies to share her story with our group. These two things made it all very real to our group. For the entire time we were at Gilgal Val suspended the regular schedule of her ladies, and they worked alongside our kids. This was amazing! Our kids were able to see how we are all very much alike, and how under different circumstances we could all be right where these ladies were.

The ladies of Gilgal opened up their hearts wide to our group. One of my greatest joys as one of the leaders was to see our students and sponsors gathered in small groups visiting with the ladies and sharing about their lives. It was so life changing for everyone in our group. There came a time each afternoon when it was time to leave and move on to our next scheduled activity, our people never wanted to leave. We had purchased Atlanta City Passes for our group to do things like The World of Coke, The Georgia Aquarium, CNN, College Football Hall of Fame and more, but our people didn't get to do all of those attractions because we didn't get back in time each day, and no one complained a single time. On Friday night we got to do a concert at Victory Outreach which is just a couple of blocks from Gilgal. This really wasn't a concert, it was a worship service! This concert was without a doubt one of the most moving experiences of my life. The ladies of Gilgal were in attendance to worship with us. What an experience!

When the service was over, our entire group was in tears and no one wanted to leave. Our people were changed from their experiences at Gilgal. This is my 16ᵗʰ year to be a high school choir sponsor and every year we go to a different location for our choir tour/mission trip. This was without a doubt the greatest experience of my life. We were so blessed by the ladies of Gilgal. We also were blessed to work with Cheryl and Deborah and to see their unconditional love for these ladies and for the Lord. Then, Ms. Val, what can I say? I know I have a lifelong friend in Atlanta,

Georgia. Ms. Val is one of the most amazing people I have ever met. Her love and devotion for her Lord and Savior Jesus Christ is so evident in everything she says or does. I just love this lady. Thank you, Val, for letting the Pioneer Drive Baptist Church High School Choir serve at Gilgal and even more so thank you for allowing us to be a part of your family! Oh, one more thing, that inch. We got Val's office painted during our stay! One of the projects we had while we were there was to paint the outside brick of the sanctuary. Our paint group worked tirelessly painting the building. On Friday as it was getting closer to time for us to wrap things up the back of the building still wasn't painted. The discussion was held whether to paint it or not since it wouldn't be seen by anyone and one of our students stepped up and said "I don't want us to be that group that leaves that inch!" Needless to say, they got that back side of the sanctuary painted before we left. I love Gilgal!

KADE P: STUDENT

A couple of months ago I had the absolute privilege to do mission work with a group of ladies at Gilgal, Inc. One of the very first days our group was there, I had the opportunity to share my testimony. I was unsure about this considering I had only met a few of the women, but I am so glad God let me open up the way I did. I learned stories that have inspired me and felt love in a whole new way that I did not know I would have received.

I saw God in each one of the ladies I worked with, and to this day I think back to that life changing week of building fences, planting gardens, painting the church walls, getting to know the ladies personally, and so so much more. I am encouraged that a group of high school students could be influenced so much in such a short time by some of the strongest, most willed, free spirited, beautiful and Christian women I have ever met. Thank you, Women of Gilgal, for giving me light on a whole new world of tough I didn't know existed!

LAURA J: STUDENT

The Gilgal women inspired me by their stories about their challenges and desires to change their lives and direction. They were so positive and have such sweet spirits. I loved working alongside them in the garden, cleaning the baseboards and windows, and washing curtains and putting them back up for one of the houses. We built relationships with each other that we will never forget. I'm so glad to know them! They have inspired me and encouraged me to stay strong in my walk with the Lord and have shown that God is always with us. Serving others together brought us all incredible joy!

ANNIE W: STUDENT

Pioneer Drive's most recent high school choir tour to Atlanta played a major role in my walk with Christ. I was very fortunate to be given the opportunity to work with my group at Gilgal. I got to help wash and paint the church with other students and a couple of the women. It was so great to work alongside these amazing women and hear their stories. Most of them had bizarre and tragic events happen in their lives, yet they remain optimistic, faithful, and grateful to God for saving them. Their love for the Lord and life was contagious and inspiring. It was truly a blessing to worship with them as friends and sisters in Christ. My time with the women of Gilgal not only allowed me to strengthen my relationship with them and the other students, but also strengthened my relationship with Christ.

MADDIE Y: STUDENT

I had the amazing opportunity to volunteer at Gilgal recovery center in Atlanta, Georgia. My experience here was not only life changing for the incredible women, which we call warriors, but it was also life changing for myself. My group's mission was to paint Gilgal's only church, which was not only messy but also incredibly entertaining. Throughout all the slinging paint and multiple brush strokes, I personally got to hear some of the women's stories of physical abuse, drug and alcohol addiction, and even sexual assault. Even with all of their struggles and heartbreak, they all seemed to keep saying how they were led back to God by his unconditional love and forgiveness through it all. Having the chance to actually work and be around all the personal, horrifying life stories opened my eyes to the fact that even if we go through the worst and darkest experiences, God will be at the end of it all. This experience has also conveyed to me that not only will he be standing with his arms stretched wide with grace and mercy, but also to give us that second, third, and even fourth chance to live in the light of the kingdom.

TARA D: STUDENT

My experience at Gilgal consisted of power washing and painting the outside of the church building, painting Val's office, washing the cars, and helping with other odd jobs. I got a chance to work with several of the ladies. They were just as willing, if not more, to help complete all the tasks. One thing that I noticed repeatedly was the desire of the women to create relationships with us as well as God. It inspires me to show Christ through everything I am doing even when my circumstances are not ideal.

CALEB E: STUDENT

I was blessed with the opportunity to work at Gilgal on my church's high school choir tour. My list of jobs included building a fence, mowing the lawns, cleaning out a shed, picking up leaves, power washing different things, and helping all the other groups with their projects. Not only did we work *for* Gilgal, we worked *with* Gilgal. The women worked alongside us, sharing their stories as they did. Our last time seeing the women was at a Friday night worship service. As I stood up there singing in worship with the women and the congregation, I realized that even though these women had made bad decisions, they still worshiped the same God I did. Even though they had sinned, there was redemption. Even though I may make mistakes that don't bring as many earthly consequences as the ones the women made, I still needed the same, sweet redemption that God has offered us. This is the testimony the women of Gilgal showed me.

ABBY D: STUDENT

This summer was my last choir tour, and I was blessed with the opportunity to work at Gilgal for four days. Like any other mission trip I'd done before, I expected my group to work hard, show Jesus to others, and go home; however, the hard work we put in, painting or working in the garden, was done alongside the girls of Gilgal. Soon, I was overwhelmed with how Jesus showed Himself to me through the women of Gilgal and the work we were doing. I worked with a young woman named Samantha. Our first day of work was only Samantha's fourth day on the campus. In our first conversations, she immediately opened up to me about her situation and her determination to find Jesus through it all. Not only were the ladies determined to work hard, but as the week progressed, they showed us how vulnerable they were to worship our Heavenly Father. This was truly a humbling experience and created in me a true motivation for raw worship and to work always with determination.

ZACHARY V: STUDENT

The day we got to Gilgal I didn't know what to expect. I imagined it as a place filled with gross women who were different in every way from my friends and me. I knew from the second we arrived at Gilgal that I was very wrong. The women of Gilgal welcomed us in with open arms and gave us a tour the first day. Over the couple of following days, I got to know the women there through working with them on many projects. The ladies there all shared their stories with us and it became impossible to not love these women. I walked away with an entirely different perspective on people in those dark times in their lives.

JACK L: STUDENT

This summer I got to work at Gilgal while on a mission trip with our church high school choir. While there I built a fence, did lawn work, built a patio, and organized a storage building. The experience that I had was amazing. I came to Gilgal expecting to minister to the women, but I quickly came to realize that they were going to be ministering to me. The way that the women treated us and each other, as well as the genuine relationship that they had with Jesus made us feel welcome and loved. The time that I spent at Gilgal changed my life, and I will never forget the women of Gilgal.

ASHLEE R: STUDENT

I am one of the students from Pioneer Drive Baptist Church that recently visited Gilgal this past summer. Now I can confidently say that going into this week of mission work and worship, I was scared yet hopeful of what that week would bring for me and my fellow choir members. We were told that we were there to do mission work and that each of us had an assigned job, but I believe we were there for more than that. During that week I was in charge of cleaning out the shed and the storage pod, along with cleaning the backyard and painting the inside of the house. Needless to say, I did a lot of different things that week, but those things weren't just assigned jobs, they were jobs that showed our love for the Lord and the love we have for others. They were also jobs that showed how we can and how we should praise the Lord through the smallest things in life. That week brought me more faith and trust in the Lord than any other trip I have been a part of. What I experienced during those four days of work was that I not only helped the girls in a huge way, but that they helped me in an even bigger way. Those girls helped me realize how I take my life for granted and that it can change in the blink of an eye. I think that in having the girls and Ms. Val show me their love, they changed me forever. They changed my outlook on my life and how the Lord is always there for me no matter what I do. Those girls showed me to always have hope, courage and faith in the Lord and because of that I am forever grateful of the time I was able to share with them.

BLAYRE O: STUDENT

I was given the opportunity to work alongside the women of Gilgal this past summer. I was a part of the church painting crew, who worked with residents Lori and Yulondor. While painting a church for four straight days might be a little grueling at times, our team was always supporting and building one another up. While at Gilgal, I learned so many things, but learning how to put aside my troubles and show the Lord's light was the biggest thing I took home with me. These women may have had a rough past, and challenging futures, but Lori and Yulondor were always smiling, laughing, encouraging, and never for one minute let their past get in the way of loving on all of us. So with all of the lessons I learned while working at Gilgal, following the example these ladies gave to us on how to shine God's light and love in everything, no matter what the circumstance, encouraged me to be a light just like the beautiful women of Gilgal every day.

GRIFFIN J: STUDENT

My time at Gilgal changed my life and my perspective on faith and trials The women there are beautiful individuals who have simply made a few bad decisions; they're no different than anyone else, no different even from myself and my fellow choir members. The love and passion they showed for Jesus and for us was almost breathtaking and working alongside them was a true blessing. I personally was somewhat isolated from the group, as I was in the Stage 2 house with Jack S replacing ceiling tiles; this was a unique blessing, however, because I could feel the love these women gave us in the smallest ways. I talked to several of the women one-on-one while working and got an insight into their life and their faith. The experience rekindled my faith and reignited my passion for God, and for that I will always love and be indebted to Gilgal.

JASE H: STUDENT

God changed my life in so many eye opening ways when we arrived at Gilgal. A couple of fellow choir members and I had the honor of remodeling a new office for Cheryl. We gutted the room, painted, installed a ceiling fan, and put new carpet in. Working beside the ladies was so amazing, but knowing what they've been through is what really hit me. Because of this intense experience, I have come to realize how blessed I truly am and how God's love never gives up. I am redeemed.

JACK S: ADULT SPONSOR

"We are all only one step away from needing a place like this." This is how Ms. Val introduced us to the ministry of Gilgal. The more we worked, the more time we spent with the women of Gilgal, the closer to home that statement hit. My team and I were blessed to have a small part in preparing an office for Ms. Cheryl, an office that will be used for counseling, mentoring, loving, and most importantly leading women closer to Christ. Life- changing? Yes! This time makes me ask daily, "In whom is my foundation, ensuring my next step is not one that leads me to Gilgal?" That foundation is Jesus! Lord, please continue to bring women, and men, to you through the ministry of Gilgal.

LANIE W: ADULT SPONSOR

I am a High School Choir Sponsor for Pioneer Drive Baptist Church's High School Choir. I was part of the group that had the honor of working at Gilgal. This experience was a tremendous blessing for me personally. As a mother of two boys I was immediately drawn in and connected with other women who were also mothers. Having this in common brought us to a level of great compassion that we shared for our children. The drive within these women to recover and follow through was touching and honest. A deep love for God and a deep yearning to do better and succeed was evident. Working together alongside these women was refreshing and encouraging. We planted flowers, creating a beautiful area surrounding the Gilgal sign, I had fun creating a craft board and message area, and also was able to work with a group painting Ms. Val's office ALL THE WAY TO THE CEILING! It was a very special time that I will always treasure

SHARYN L: ADULT SPONSOR

My visit to Gilgal was with PDBC High School choir during the summer of 2016. Since January, we had heard about Gilgal and the special people of Gilgal. Our time there was spent working alongside these ladies to get some much needed work done on their campus. The time we shared was precious and will never be forgotten. The ladies shared openly about how they ended up at Gilgal and how their lives were being changed because they were there. The power of the Lord was evident as I could see HOPE in each lady. Despite their previous circumstances, their lives were being renewed through daily Bible study and the outpouring love of the Gilgal ministry team. I was inspired to look at others with a different heart after leaving Gilgal. I now see those with troubled lives as people who need

God's love poured into them. God is blessing the work at Gilgal!

ROSIE H: ADULT SPONSOR

At Gilgal, our youth witnessed the brokenness of this world infiltrating the hearts of women as they shared testimonies of their struggles and brokenness which lead to addiction and pain. However, they also witnessed Jesus mending, reconciling, and redeeming the brokenness through the staff and volunteers who refused to give up or count them out. God does his work of redemption through relationships; our relationship with Him and our relationships with others. My awareness of this truth became more profound as I grew to love and admire the strength of the women I came to know. Our youth were inspired as they experienced God's love through relationships which bore the marks of humanity's bruising and the redemption of God's love. It was a joy and pleasure for me to see the eyes of our youth transformed to see like Jesus as they interacted with the ladies of Gilgal.

SAMANTHA P., CURRENT CLIENT

For most people, being 10 years old is significant for many triv-ial reasons: "double-digits," finishing elementary school, and starting to figure out who you are without your parents' help. For Samantha, a frank, but joyful woman with a personality the size of Texas, her 10th year of life was marked by her first time using drugs and her first time being molested by her 13-year-old step-sister.

For most of her adolescent life, Samantha had only known vi-olence, abuse, and drugs. Her older step-sister, who Samantha bluntly described as psychotic, would torture Samantha and Samantha's younger sister, forcing them to bend to her will, which is what eventually led to Samantha's drug use. "[My step-sister] gave me my first cigarette, my first drink, my first blunt, my first hit of cocaine…it was her," she says. "She told us she'd kill us if we didn't. We'd wake up and she'd have a butcher knife to our throats."

There was no safe haven for Samantha at her biological father's house either. "[He] was extremely volatile," she says. "He has a lot of money, he's very powerful, and he's very mean… He's a very sick man." So, Samantha's years consisted of a cycle of beatings from her brothers and father for three months at her father's home in Minnesota and being tortured and molested by her psychotic step-sister. Additionally, Samantha was struggling with a strained relationship between herself, her biological mother, and her step-father. Her birth father had threatened to kill Saman-tha's mother and step-father if she chose to show them any emotion other than hate. "It was a pretty hostile environment for most of my life," she says.

This trauma continued in Samantha's life: her drug use escalated, she was raped, and she lost five babies in miscarriages. All of this stole Samantha's childhood from her. Fifth grade graduation didn't stand a chance as a milestone between all of the other horrific events in Samantha's life. Eventually, Samantha found herself sleeping under a bridge in Downtown Atlanta, which is where she realized she wasn't living the life she was supposed to be living. "I surrendered everything to God," she says. "I said God, 'this is not me, this is not my life…it's not who I am.'"

While she was living under the bridge, Samantha made the acquaintance of another woman, who happened to have spent a few nights at Gilgal. The two women had spent months talking to each other under the bridge, but Gilgal had never come up. As soon as the other woman described Gilgal to Samantha, Samantha knew she had to find a way to get to Gilgal. She was so determined to acquire a bed that she completed her required tuberculosis and syphilis tests by herself within two days. "I was not playing," she says.

Despite her determination to get to Gilgal, once she spent her first night, Samantha started to have anxiety. "I had a full-blown panic attack and anxiety attack, all wrapped in one," she says. "I was freaking out. I had to start dealing with things: emotions, reality, the things I had done and said, and I was just like no…no, no, no," she says, shaking her head and laughing. Since her first night, Samantha has packed her bags on three separate occasions, but each time she was ready to walk out, Ms. Cheryl was there to stop her. "[Ms. Cheryl] is one of God's very special people," she says. "She gives you this euphoric feeling… I firmly believe she is one of God's disciples."

When Samantha was ready to leave because of a misunderstanding with a false positive on one of her drug tests, Ms. Cheryl took to time to make sure Samantha didn't have a chance to leave, even though it meant "kidnapping" her and driving around Atlanta for an hour and a half to talk with her and pray with her. After much frustration and many threats to leave, Samantha's doctor called Gilgal to inform her that her previous comment that the pills could not produce a false positive was incorrect, and Samantha was able to remain at Gilgal. "[God] worked a miracle," she says.

As she's been at Gilgal, Samantha's trust in God has grown. When she first walked through Gilgal's doors, Samantha confessed to Ms. Cheryl that she didn't think she would ever be able to trust God when she couldn't even trust her own mom, but through her time at Gilgal, God has used multiple situations to show Samantha that He is someone she can trust in. He has shown her through the incident with her false positive test, by bringing her to Gilgal, and through a situation with a roommate. Over and over, God has proved to Samantha that she can release herself to Him, and she has.

He has provided the sanctuary that Samantha never had when she was just a kid. "I firmly believe I wouldn't be alive if Gilgal hadn't taken me in," she says. She describes Gilgal as God's paradise, a safe haven where she can grow closer to Jesus, learn His will for her, and heal from all of the pain she has faced in the past. "I thought getting off the drugs was going to be the hardest part…no," she says. "The hardest part is dealing with everything that I have bottled up, pushed down, not dealt with, emotions I've never experienced before…I've always dealt with everything in anger for fear of being hurt." Although every day hasn't been just another day in paradise, Samantha is just happy to be in a place where she can be guarded both physically and spiritually. "For the first time in my life, I feel safe."

20 August 2016

HOLLY G., GRADUATE

I'm a Gilgal woman and I know that without God and the staff and volunteers at Gilgal I would have never made it. I was a junkie, hooked on meth, living from place to place. My little brother found Gilgal and brought me there. I was so messed up in the head and afraid. But I walked in the door and all I got was love from the beginning.

I had no hope until Gilgal showed me how much Jesus loved me. Jesus opened up the door and showed me that I am his masterpiece. My addiction to drugs was only believing the Devil's lie. The love from Jesus shows me more new and amazing things every day.

In my time at Gilgal I learned to live with different kind of personalities and that was hard. Ms. Val would tell us that it is easy to love a person that is easy to love, but Jesus said to love everyone, even the ones that are not so easy. I had a person in there that was driving me crazy and she would tell me to pray for her. I thought, "someone else should pray for her." I wanted to beat her up. But one night I did pray for her, really prayed from my heart. You know, Jesus showed me. He answered my prayers. She got up that morning and was nice to me. All I could say was, thank you Jesus.

There were so many other times He showed me that there is power in prayer. God gave us Ms. Val to show us love of Jesus just where we were. I am still clean and serving him every day. I'm not perfect, but I'm saved by his blood. Thank you, Ms. Val and all the ones there that work and volunteer there. I would not be here without all of you who love Jesus right where we are. Thank you.

I owe my life to Jesus and Gilgal for not giving up on me. I love each and every one of the staff, volunteers, graduates, and clients. I pray for all the girls I don't even know that I know will be touched in so many ways.

13 July 2016

THE JACKSONS, VOLUNTEERS

Barbara J. and her daughter, Catherine J., learned about Gilgal when Catherine had her December 2013 piano recital there. At the request of a client, she started teaching piano lessons in January 2014. Barbara has also become involved with Gilgal, serving as a member of the Board. Below, Barbara and Catherine interview each other about their involvement with Gilgal. Naitnaphit L. poses questions and clarifications from time to time.

BJ: So when we first went to Gilgal, that very first day, what was your initial reaction? What did you first think?

CJ: Well, I was really nervous to go. I don't know if you remember that, but I was clinging to you pretty much, and I was planning on not interacting with the women because at the shelters, I mean it's not really a shelter...

BJ: But that had been your previous experience.

CJ: And, at church when we would go, there were always the nice people that were kind of the exception, but I had always known homeless people and people recovering from drug addictions to be harsher, so I was nervous that it was going to be like that when we walked in, and then Ms. Val was all like "okay! We're going to mix and mingle! Everyone sit next to a client and clients sit next to the piano players," and I was like, "oh, I really don't think so, like, okay, sure..." But,

then, I remember I went up there and played, and I think I messed up bunch, and they came up to me afterwards because I was the oldest one there, and they were like, "oh my gosh, that was amazing," and they were gushing, and I was like, "These women are really nice and they want to get to know me." It was very much the opposite of what I expected...which, I guess my first impression would be, it's not what I expected it to be, which is a good thing.

CJ: What about you?

BJ: I remember your piano teacher inviting you to go, and they sent us a list of things we could bring and I remember thinking, okay, we're going to this shelter, let me get some things, and I wanted to participate and bring, you know, I think I got some cleaning products, but I remember thinking, okay, it's Saturday, okay. Like, it was more of an obligation we had to fulfil. I wasn't walking in that day thinking "wow, I'm really excited about what Gilgal is and how we can get involved." I had no intention of walking out of there and feeling involved.

But, opposite of you, when we walked in, there was a woman, who, I know she graduated from the program, but I don't remember her name, but I remembered, kind of, the musicians were sitting on one side and the Gilgal women were sitting on the other, and I remember thinking I didn't like that at all. I remember walking in and feeling the presence of God there, like something drew me right in, and I know exactly who the woman was, and I went and sat down next to her and just started having a conversation with her, and I felt at that moment that God was already working in my heart, that something was already going on. She ended up *crying* through the entire concert.

CJ: That's what I forgot to say -- they were all crying.

BJ: They were so emotional, and, um, I wish I could remember her name, and I know Val would know her because she was our graduate. She ended up giving us our tour when we went back and had to sit down with Val and go over all of the rules. She gave us our tour, because she was almost -- towards the end of the program, and I remember there was a family that had, like, a baby sitting in front of me and her, and she just kept crying and wanting to play with the baby. Then later on, Val had said that they don't interact with children that much, unless it's a friends and family day.

I just remembered walking in and , now that I'm talking about it, I was transformed almost as soon as I walked in. And I, at other times, have gone to shelters and other, you know, volunteer opportunities, and have left there thinking, oh, that's something I'd like to do. Gilgal is really the only place that I have stayed committed to and really that involved with.

"I REMEMBER WALKING IN AND FEELING THE PRESENCE OF GOD THERE."

CJ: I remember when we started talking to them, I was like, oh, this is really different.

BJ: Yes.

CJ: And then they all cried during Elizabeth's song, when she sang, and they were *all* crying, like every single one.

BJ: What was that song?

CJ: It was something she wrote. It was about, I don't think it was intentional, but it happened to be really relatable for them, and I was, like, oh, this is not at all...

BJ: She was like a thirteen-year-old girl…

CJ: She was in my performance group, and she performed it, she sang it…

BJ: and the song was about, it was heavy.

CJ: (laughs) Yeah, we were, like, "how did a thirteen year old write this?"

BJ: It was about being changed, and transformed, overcoming and not being seen. The women were all moved by it. It was a really special day. It was really neat.

CJ: Yeah, it was.

BJ: What's been your favorite experience since we've been at Gilgal?

CJ: I feel like, before this, like the book and everything, my experience was piano. So, I guess when they would 'get it' because I never knew if I was doing -- because I had never taught before and it's not like math where you can just illustrate it. I feel like music can be hard to teach sometimes and I didn't know if I was doing a good job, and I didn't know if I was connecting with the women, or if they liked having me come. But then, after the first few classes, they were all asking questions and really excited. If I was teaching someone a harder piece that wasn't in the book, like Ashley wanted to play the "Little Drummer Boy," and she got it. I guess when they "got it."

They got so excited too, like when

they had the opportunity to play in front of people, when we would do recitals and everything, and when the had the opportunity to show off and b the star for a second, they got so excited! I could tell that it meant a lot to them that I cared to teach them piano because a lot of them would say "this is cool. I didn't think I could ever do something like this, but here am, playing piano in front of all of these people, giving a recital," so I guess that's my favorite experience.

CJ: That was one of my questions fo you too: what's your favorite part of Gilgal, or being at Gilgal?

BJ : I think the best part about being there is just that you get a glimpse of seeing how God can work in people's lives. I use this example a lot, but remember Ashley H. and how much acne she had? She would, um, go under her hoodie and she'd have her zip up jacket and be rocking back and forth and she wouldn't want to participate in the lessons. And that was when we were going every Saturday, and then we walked in that one Saturday and all of a sudden her acne was cleared up, she was all bright, and she had said she'd found Jesus and she wanted to play the piano. I think that was really the first time how I saw that God's power is just, you know, limitless and just being able to see the transformation right before our very eyes, in somebody else. It was like a miracle.

CJ: What's like the hardest part?

BJ: Oh gosh, I remember when the first girl left -- I cried and cried.

CJ & BJ: Jessica

BJ: I remember when Val sat down with us and she said, you know, people are going to leave, and that's going to be really hard, and I will never for-get that first year, when women left, I was so emotional and just had a really hard time with it. And, then over time, as Val would say, you know, God uses that person who walks out the door -- and as a reminder we always talk about -- the girl that asked for the piano lessons wasn't there when we came to back to teach, but look at, by her just being there, and we've seen that so many times. And that doesn't mean, I think some of them, yes, they do leave and return to their previous lives.

And I think for some of them, they've come and they've heard the Gospel and they've come to know Jesus. But that's hard, when they leave and it's still crushing when they don't make it.

BJ: Me again?

CJ: (giggling) I just asked you one!

BJ: So, our relationship and going to Gilgal together…

CJ: Yeah

BJ: How do you feel about that and how that's been impacted?

CJ: Like our relationship?

BJ: Yeah, just as you and I going together?

CJ: I feel like, we don't have many... we like a lot of the same stuff and we like watching movies together and listening to music and going to Broadway shows. But there's never anything that we did together. It wasn't like, oh! Like, let's go play soccer. There was never an activity we did together. Just because I feel like we were interested... As a kid, I wasn't interested in the stuff you were interested in. But, I feel like it's given us something, not like, oh now we have something to do together, but it's something special that we do together. It's been fun. I like when I go and they talk about you. And they're like, "I love your mom," and I'm like "Me too, I do too, she's pretty great."

And then, I like seeing a different side of you, like not you as a mom. When you talk to the women, you're still my mom and you still have the same character traits and everything, but you're not being a mom to them, you're being a friend and a mentor, and it's cool to see you out of your usual context.

BJ: And it's the same thing. I remember when you stood up and gave your first piano lesson I was like "oh my gosh, she can do that, wow." And I know from being your mom how accomplished and how able you are, but then to see that in action, and then to see God working in your life through that, and I just always thought it was so fun that way we each had a role when we got there. I think it's a great way God orchestrated it that I don't play the piano, so, that's not a gift of mine, that's not something I can offer, so being the controlling person that I am I had to completely surrender that to you. And it was such a blessing to do that, to say, that's yours, and I'll do the brownies and the chips and dips and the Coke, and do what I like to do, which is to fellowship with the women.

CJ: It's a place where we can both do what we like, but be together.

Except sometimes I think they like you better than me (cute smile).

BJ: Nooo, we're equally loved.

CJ: What's it like being on the board? How did you come to be on the board?

BJ: So, um, well, so after you and I started going on a regular basis and obviously knew that this was something I was going to be very involved with, Val

asked me to chair the Gala last October and, by doing that and getting more involved and getting to know Val more and the other board members...

I think it was in the middle of planning that [the Gala], Val and I were on the phone one day and she said that a couple of the board members had mentioned to her why don't we ask Barbara to be on the board. And I was like, "what, me, a board member? No."

And I think that's a lot, just personally speaking on a spiritual level, I think that it's a lot of what God's blessed me with at Gilgal. It's taken away a lot of I'm no good, I'm not adequate, like, I'm not worthy, or oh gosh, no, that's somebody else far more godly and capable than me; that's one thing that I think I've grown spiritually and matured. Where He has you, He has you. Just keep moving forward with that. So, just saying yes to that and then being on the board.

One of the things I think is really near about being on the board is that the ladies know that I'm on the board and I think that gives them...They know I'm invested in them personally.

CJ: You're not just going in and out.

BJ: That I'm committed, and I think that really means something to them.

BJ: What are some ways you think you've grown spiritually at Gilgal or has your time there changed your relationship with Jesus?

"THEY REMIND ME I NEED TO BE BETTER."

CJ: Yes it has. I guess it's more, I kind of, with the women, I went through the same thing they went through when they get there. I mean, I always knew that I could trust God with everything. But it's so hard not to do that when you're watching all of these amazing things happen, and now especially hearing all of these stories about these times where they just "let go and let God" and were just trusting in God and praying about it. I guess it just made me want to be more reliant on Him.

Being around them has also given me hope. If I'm living the life I'm living -- I go to a good school, I have a roof over my head, I'm eating good food every day, like, I can participate in activities, I'll be able to go to a good college next year if I want to, like if I have a privileged life and these women who society is always like "Oh, they're the lowest of the low, like they don't have anything," and yet they're so joyful, like, why can't I be like that? Like, I need to be like that. If I'm going to say that I'm a Christian then I need to act like it, and being around them reminds me that I need to be better and like a better example of my faith.

When I'm struggling I think of the women at Gilgal and how hard their lives have been, and *yet,* like I was telling you yesterday, we were listening to Samantha's story, and she came in and she was laughing and having a good time, and it doesn't *surprise me*, because I get it, she's here now, she's experiencing the love of Jesus, but that still amazes me, and I want to be more

like that, and I want people to see that in me.

BJ: (crying) It's a big thing. I think God's given us a gift. A lot of people won't, and I remember feeling that way, like I wanted to do something, but it never felt right, and I think we've been obedient to his calling. I think he opened a door and we said yes. And that is just talking about strengthening your faith, where you can just continually see…

And that's one of the things about being around Val that's just impacted me -- her faith is so deep and solid and she trusts. It's just encouraged me, even when just planning the event or the Gala, just to say I know God has this, and He does, and, like you said, putting that in your personal life as well.

CJ: So as a board member, what do you want to see happen at Gilgal in the future? What are your hopes for Gilgal?

BJ: If you had asked me that question a year ago I might say, "oh let's fill the beds and get more women in," but one thing I've seen this year, because we'll only graduate one person this year, is that it doesn't matter if we're graduating one person, 25, 50, or 100, that just by being there and doing God's work and being true to Him and His calling, that lives are changed. Your life is changed, my life is changed, countless people. The lives of the women. My goal is that we always stay true to God's calling and not to compromise Him for more beds. There are things we can do as a nonprofit to get more money in the door, but you have to make concession for that.

I pray that as we bring on new board members that have the same goals as we do, but that we would grow.

I would like to see the building upgraded and improved and physical changes, but as long as we stay anchored to who we are then we're doing a great job.

BJ: Is there a favorite experience or person?

CJ: I was going to talk about this. I like when I get to know one of the women a little extra. Not just because "oh, I really like her, she's my favorite," like, we just happen to click and get along.

Like with Ashley D, I just love her. At times I felt like she was my older sister. We were around a lot with that group, she was always joking with me, and I remember that was March, spring of sophomore year and I was showing them pictures and they were like, Catherine, you need to wear a longer dress! (My dress wasn't that short), but it was just like, oh they're looking out for me.

When I make a special relationship like that, it's really cool. I'm Facebook friends with them and I like to see what they're up to. I want to keep in touch with them. Like, when I called Tiffany the other day, it was just like "hey how's it going?!" Just chatting, catching up. I've already seen with a few women in this group, like with Semesterlia, the new girl, I loved her,

I was like, oh this girl, we could be friends, and just getting the connection with the women.

Of course I love all of them, but it's like friends, you get closer to others and it's really fun having that bond with specific people and knowing they're looking forward to you coming and asking about you and keeping tabs on you and looking out for you because they're all older than me, like I said Ashley is like my sister I felt like at times. It's cool to see that kind of relationship.

BJ: I think that, now that you're talking about that, it's reminding me, I can't remember who said it, but I remember when we first started going the women would comment that just by you and me being there together that it was like modeling a mother-daughter relationship, like I want that relationship with my daughter. They had no role models or nothing to base anything off, they were being given cigarettes and alcohol and drug at such a young age, so now that you're mentioning that, I think a lot of them enjoying our friendship is the same thing.

CJ: Which I think is cool too. I know we have a good relationship, but a lot of my friends have good relationships with their moms, but when [the women] comment on it, I realize just how good I have it with you. A lot of people don't have that relationship. You're like my friend and my mom.

(Fist bump)

BJ: I know at this point in your life you're not drinking, you're not using drugs. Do you think being there and seeing what drugs and alcohol and sex and prostitution can do to somebody, do you feel like that's for them, has that impacted you?

CJ: (nodding) Yes! Yesterday, Semesterlia said it -- she was just having a rough time, she started drinking when she was 33 years old. She was like, "I was just out at a friend's birthday party, and I just ordered a drink, and I realized when I was drinking it I wasn't sad anymore." And I was like, that's so scary. She wasn't even trying to drown out the pain and it just happened and it led her into the spiral. She wasn't even looking for something to numb herself. She just happened to be out at a party. She's 33 years old, like 33 year olds have a drink to be social. She said, I drank it and was like "oh, that's what this is about." You don't know what effect it will have on you until you have a drink, you don't know what it's going to do to you.

I've always been like that, but it just reinforced it, I don't want to get into that pattern, ever. That also reminds me, back to the whole like faith thing -- I don't ever want to get to the point where a drink makes me feel better. I want to make sure I stay grounded, and stay focused on God and know that no matter how bad things get it doesn't have to be that bad. Like I want to be able to go out and have a drink (when I'm older) without it being a highlight.

NL: Elaborate on it connecting back to God.

CJ: I mean, I haven't had a hard life; I'm seventeen years old, but when I've had experiences with people, or relationships, and I've been down on myself, I have remind myself to go back because as a Christian I can't get caught up in myself. I always remind myself that there's a bigger plan in place and that always gives me hope, and I want to make sure I always stay hopeful, so I don't get to a point where I hit rock bottom because there's not really a rock bottom. It could always be worse, and it's not going to last forever, so I don't want to get to the point where I'm wallowing, like I'm never going to get out of this, to the point where if I do have a sip of alcohol everything is going to magically feel better.

BJ: Very mature response.

BJ: How do you see yourself moving forward with the women? I feel like we haven't been down there for piano in a while.

CJ: And that makes me sad.

BJ: Makes me sad too.

CJ: I like hanging out with them on the fourth of July; that's fun.

BJ: That's been some of my favorite, to be honest.

CJ: In the future it depends where I go to school. If I went somewhere closer, I want to see if i can make the time at last one weekend a month to spend time with them. Because I don't want to stop. It's become a huge part of my...I've written every community service paper about Gilgal. I like talking about it.

I want people to know about it because I've had such a good experience there and I love it so much

I don't want to stop just because I'm going to college, so I want to keep, as often as I can, and it depends on where I go. If I can't be there I want another me to be there and continue because I feel like they get a lot out of piano. Of course I love spending time with them and I know they love spending time with me, but I know piano is something special to them. It gives them confidence, like "I didn't know I could do this, like I love this so much." I want them to have that even if I'm not there.

BJ: Because it's so different from the other activities they have there. It's just a total diversion. After the piano recital, they get up there and play "Mary Had a Little Lamb" and it's, wow, look what I just did. I don't know if you know this or not, at the first recital we brought a little potted rose plant, Ashley D still has hers, so she, it's been about two years, she's tended to it, graduated, lived at Gilgal for a while, planted it now, and it's thriving.

I love that. It's back to what's your goal for Gilgal. Look at the way her life's been changed. It's all God.

CJ: Anything I didn't ask you that you want to talk about?

BJ: points -- I love you!

NL: What do you want others to know about GIlgal?

CJ: In my community service papers I always focus on and highlight the stereotype of these women is so wrong, it is so not what you would expect.

They're real people, they have real emotions, they've been through real stuff. They're some of the most amazing people that I've met in my life, and so many people would never think that. Unfortunately, it has a connotation with it and people just think…

I feel like part of it is Gilgal, it's just like special there, it's SO NOT what people would expect it to be. Don't just assume because they have a label.

BJ: I agree with you completely. Some of the most amazing women I've met, I've met there. I would echo every-thing you said. It's authentic. You know what, change happens at Gilgal (laughs).

CJ: It works.

BJ: Everybody has a story at Gilgal. Every volunteer, every board member every woman that comes in. Change happens. That's all I can say.

CJ: What's something about Ms. Val or something she always says...

BJ: The most impactful thing is when she says it doesn't matter how long someone spends time there. We've seen examples of that with the girl who asked to play piano. The girl who came in and told Katrice about the job I'm fairly certain that the woman who referred Samantha, she was at Gilgal for two nights. Her day and a half -- don't think she stayed the full week. I had a very impactful conversation with her that changed me spiritually.

Michelle came, right when we were doing to Gala last year, gave her testimony, said she was just happy to have a pillow under her head that night. She left, that day or the next day, if it's the same Michelle.

CJ: It makes sense with the timeline.

BJ: Michelle had said she was homeless and living under a bridge, sleeping on chairs. Just when you told me that -- that's just more, right there. And she tells everybody that comes through that door that she loves them. (Crying) The impact of those *words*, you hear I love you how many times a day. You know you're loved. And you know you're loved by the Lord, and that was Michelle, she kept saying I'm not worthy, and I think that's a lot of the reason why she left. She felt she wasn't worthy to be there, and just by having that conversation with her and looking in her in the eye and telling her she's worthy reminded me that I'm worthy that He died for me. And if I am, it's a gift for everybody, it's not just a gift for somebody special.

NL: We're all special because He loves us.

BJ: It's unbelievable.

CJ: What I want people to know about Gilgal, if you were ever doubting in your faith, just spend two hours there.

BJ: Five minutes

CJ: (laughing) Yeah. If you were ever questioning, just go and see what it's about and I feel like you would know.

BJ: It's authentic. I've brought women, solid believers there. Who just walked in the door and opened up the door and walked in and said there's something here. Don't walk in if you don't want to walk out a changed person.

NL: It's true.

4 August 2016

TIFFANY M., GRADUATE

For Tiffany M., finding real, honest love was never an easy task. From a young age, she was sexually abused by her uncle and was constantly exposed to drugs and alcohol by her alcoholic father. Her house was a house of "sex, drugs, and rock and roll," she says.

As a result of her traumatic childhood, Tiffany became sexually active at a very young age. She graduated high school when she was eight months pregnant with her first daughter and had her second daughter soon after. Because of her home situation, Tiffany had easy access to drugs and used during both pregnancies. Eventually, her second husband had her children removed from her care, which led to a battle with depression and a plummet in self-respect.

She started using drugs "really badly," and began sleeping around. "I was a whore," she says bluntly. "I was proud of it; I thought I was cute. Tiffany even got to a point where she thought the meth was good for her, so she kept using and sleeping around, unconcerned with the consequence her actions would bring. Ultimately, Tiffany was arrested for possession, but her best friend and eventual Gilgal graduate, Ashley D., with whom she had grown up, also happened to be in the same jail.

While she was in jail, Ashley encouraged Tiffany to start reading the Bible. So, Tiffany began to read the Word, marking it vigorously and wearing down its pages from constant use. Tiffany also was able to detox from her excessive drug use while she was in jail and realized that she didn't ever want to go back to using again. Her social worker was able to get Tiffany a spot at Gilgal, and Tiffany arrived eager to start the program

Gilgal's environment was different than anything Tiffany had expe rienced before; "I had always been around guys; Gilgal taught me how to be around women." Additionally, Gilgal played an integral role in helping Tiffany gain back the self-worth and self-respect that she had lost many years before. In fact, as soon as she graduated from the program, Gilgal helped Tiffany get her teeth replaced after all of the years of damage caused by drug use.

But between improving her relationship with women and boosting her self-worth, Gilgal also brought Tiffany closer to Jesus. "It's not about religion, it's about relationship," says Tiffany, who had always believed in God, but developed her relationship with Jesus Christ at Gilgal. "It's already been done," she says. "Works come from the fact that you love Jesus and you want to please him."

Now that she's graduated from Gilgal, Tiffany plans to focus on her happiness so she is never tempted to do drugs again. She continues to grow in her relationship with Jesus each day.

17 July 16

MS. CHERYL, STAFF

When I first began my walk with the Lord, I could never have imagined the path He would choose for me, or where it would ultimately lead me, but one thing is for sure: I am grateful for the journey (even the painful parts), and for the privilege to serve Him at Gilgal.

Many of you know Val's story of Gilgal's founding in 2005 and how the name was chosen from the story of Joshua leading the children of Israel into Canaan. After crossing the Jordan River, they took 12 stones from the riverbed, and built an altar to remember God's deliverance from Egyptian slavery. *"Then the LORD said to Joshua, 'Today I have rolled away the reproach of Egypt from you.' So the name of that place is called Gilgal to this day"* (Joshua 5:9). Here they kept their first Passover and renewed circumcision rite. And, the tabernacle of the Lord rested in the center of this significant city.

There are other stories in the Bible where great men of faith were mentioned at Gilgal. Samuel (1 Samuel 7:16) made it one of the three places where he annually held circuit court, and Elisha for a time made it his headquarters (2 Kings 2:1; 2 Kings 4:38). And for us today, Gilgal stil represents a place of great faith because the Lord Jesus Christ still remain the center of all that we say and do.

Over the years, I have personally watched in awe as God has performed miracles in the hearts and lives of the women who come through our doors. I've also experienced Him transform and heal my own heart while serving at Gilgal. It truly is a place of healing and new beginnings for anyone open to what God has to offer. Many of the wome we serve have been through multiple addiction and recovery centers prior to coming to Gilgal, and while they can cite valuable things they have gleaned from other programs, many have shared that something was missing.

I believe that missing component is Christ. Tools and models are helpful at modifying thinking, changing behaviors, and aiding in sobriety but they can't address the heart, which is where the true transformation takes place. At Gilgal, our goal is not to help women simply get sober, or even stay clean, but it is to help women live free, through the life and power of Jesus Christ.

Galatians 5:1 says, "It was for freedom that Christ set us free." John 8:36 says, "If the son makes you free, you are free indeed!"

I pray every man, woman and child who encounters Gilgal in any way-- client, volunteer, partner, staff, will see Jesus -- Only Jesus -- in all we say and do. For He alone has the Words of Life (John 6:67) because He alone is "the Way, the Truth and the Life" (John 14:6). Change really does happen at Gilgal and I am so grateful He lets me be a small part of it!

8 September 2016

TOM W., VOLUNTEER

"Are you a Christian?"

It was August 2010, and I had been volunteering at Gilgal for about a year, working with the Board of Directors to develop a strategic plan for Gilgal's future. I was now being interviewed for a position as a board member, and as a Christ-centered nonprofit, Val Cater, the founder and Executive Director of Gilgal, wanted to make sure my religious orientation was a good fit with Gilgal's mission.

I answered "yes" to Val's question.

I identified as a Christian. I had been raised by Christian parents, occasionally taken to church and Sunday school throughout my childhood, married a Catholic woman, sent my children to Catholic schools, and even went to church from time to time. So I was a Christian.

But what kind of Christian was I? Was I a Christian in name only? Did I really walk the talk of my professed faith? Indeed, what is a Christian? I knew the media was full of famous so-called Christian leaders who espoused views that I certainly did not share. Were they Christians? Am I really a Christian? I was at a spiritual crossroads and didn't know it.

In 2007, with my kids grown and in college, I decided to return to college and get a Master's degree in Business Administration at Kennesaw State University. I already had a Master's in Public Administration, but I had always wanted an MBA and my company offered to pay most of the cost, so I said why not. Eighteen months of hard work and I'll have it, I thought. Little did I know it was the beginning of a new direction in my lifetime journey.

Part of my MBA studies included many assignments that called for self-reflection on what I wanted both professionally and personally. I was assigned a mentor, or coach, whose job was to help me through this journey. I was blessed to be assigned Dr. Paul Lopez: businessman extraordinaire, philanthropist, nonprofit leader and volunteer, college professor, devout Christian. Paul Lopez would become perhaps the most influential person of my adult life.

Through discussions with Paul, I decided that I wanted to use my business acumen and advanced education, on a volunteer basis, to help nonprofits develop strategic plans that would take their organizations to the next level. When I received my MBA in 2009, I reached out to Hands On Atlanta, a nonprofit that links up volunteers with nonprofits. Gilgal was seeking a volunteer to help them develop a strategic plan, and so a match was made. I met with Val Cater, and off to work we went with the Board of Directors to develop a strategic plan for Gilgal.

My work at Gilgal as a volunteer and board member has been a spiritual journey that has grown my faith, my understanding of what it means to be a Christian, and to be a true follower of Jesus. It is an honor and privilege to serve the women in our program and to behold in them their miraculous transformation into new lives. I believe this is the essence of Jesus's teachings: giving a loving, helpful hand to our brothers and sisters in need. I am blessed to have a front row seat to bear witness to the work of God and our Gilgal staff and our volunteers as we work together to restore homeless women with addictions.

Yes, I am indeed a Christian, and I feel like I am now pursuing God's path for me.

8 August 2016

YULONDOR F., CURRENT CLIENT

What you grow up with is what you learn to know and for Yulondor F, a faith-filled, tall woman with bright eyes and an easy laugh, that knowledge involved alcohol. Both her parents were alcoholics and she grew up in a house where "we just didn't talk about things." She was raised with manners, with a roof over her head, clothes on her back, and food in her stomach; she was raised to be polite, to go to church, with a mom who wanted "the best for us." But as a kid she started stealing her mom's liquor and then her friend's dad's corn liquor. Soon she kept seeing everyone else smoke weed, so she started doing it too. "That was all I saw. That was all I knew," she says.

Five months ago, though, she had been in and out of drugs so that she could "just forget about things" -- the things that were happening to her and the things that had happened to her as a child -- and in and out of prostitution, when she found herself in a motel room in very poor shape. She couldn't get out of bed and her head was pounding. She knew the Holy Spirit was telling her, "it's time to go. It's time to get up out of here. It's time to get yourself together and get into rehab." She was done. She called her godmother and friend to help her. She learned that her blood pressure was so high she was on the verge of a stroke. She was eventually able to get in touch with Reverend Turner, who was able to speak to Ms. Val to get her into Gilgal.

This has been Yulondor's third time in rehab and before, she "wasn't ready to use God's gifts," but she knew now that God would lead her to the right place. "The Holy Spirit had me the whole time. I didn't give it a second thought," she says. In fact, God had never left her. "I left God," she says. "You can't serve two masters. But God never went anywhere." She began to understand that the alcohol was "what my life belonged to before...and God is who my life belongs to now. My life has purpose." She starts talking faster, her eyes light up, she gestures with her hands, she smiles. She is overcome with joy.

She would like to work and serve in His ministry because "it's time I show my appreciation for Him," she says. "I've already tried it my way and that almost killed her. She now understands that "God is good and to be able to experience His goodness is a blessing. It's amazing how God

can work in your life and you turn your back on Him, but He still is there for you."

At Gilgal, she's almost like a mother to the other women, coaxing them to ask questions during classes, making sure they are outfitted well for special events, and thoughtfully going over her dinner menu when it's her turn to cook. She's ready to accept responsibility for her growth in Christ, too. She's ready to do it "the right way." In seven months it will be her turn to graduate from Gilgal and work -- she wants to give back to God and back to Gilgal. She'd like to find transitional housing and work in God's ministry. She's thankful for the love and support of her godparents and is looking forward to having a relationship with her two adult sons and her two grandchildren. The night before she left for Gilgal her youngest son started speaking to her again.

God loves Yulondor and she loves Him -- it's easy to see. "If you have a relationship with God and with the Holy Spirit, your life is never the same," she says.

28 July 2016

JESSICA P., GRADUATE

Before she came to Gilgal, Jessica P., an alternative redhead with various tattoos and piercings, didn't have a reason to believe in God. "My life was awful," she says. "Everything bad that could've happened, happened."

The bad started when Jessica was just eleven years old. Her mom had left her family and had tried to commit suicide, which tore Jessica's family apart and drove Jessica's heartbroken father, the primary caregiver, to alcoholism. Soon after Jessica's mother left, Jessica's family moved from South Georgia up to North Georgia, where a lack of a stable home allowed Jessica to quickly fall in with the wrong crowd. Jessica was suddenly experimenting with drugs, alcohol, and parties in her middle school years. She continued using drugs and alcohol as a means of entertainment throughout middle school and high school, until, when she was eighteen, she realized she was addicted. "It wasn't fun anymore," she says. "I couldn't control myself."

Eventually, Jessica was arrested for possession of methamphetamines and a violation of her probation. Following her arrest, she was placed in jail to await her sentence, but in a place that is usually barren of hope, Jessica encountered a woman named Angelica, a former Gilgal resident, who would point her towards the place that would bring Jessica continual hope, after a life of hurt and despair.

So, Jessica was released from jail and went to start Gilgal's year-long program, but it wasn't without qualms: "I was so scared on the way to Gilgal," she says. Her hesitations lingered for the first month she was at Gilgal; when she realized living a life void of structure, like she had been, was not an option in an environment that depends on routine to thrive. She soon adjusted, however, and surrendered to Gilgal; "It was like a breath of fresh air when I did what I was supposed to do," she says.

Suddenly, the girl who had grown up believing that there couldn't be a God was surrounded by the most compelling evidence that He is real and He is good: love. "The whole place is built on love," she says. The overwhelming evidence for God and Gilgal's strong roots in Christ brought Jessica close to the God, who she had believed couldn't exist.

"Reading, seeing, and feeling taught me a lot," she says. "There were times where I could actually feel [God]." Much of that love is shown through the staff, and Ms. Val in particular. "The most amazing thing is how much [the staff] care[s] about Gilgal," she says. "Ms. Val has the biggest heart; she is a God-fearing, God-loving woman. She comes off as stern and a little scary, but she's really not; she knows what's right."

Jessica completed the program and graduated from Gilgal in 2015 and is thriving. She now works two jobs (one of which was the job she had while at Gilgal) and just recently bought a house, where she lives with her boyfriend and her seven-year-old son. Even though it's been over a year since she graduated from Gilgal, Jessica still takes time to visit and talk to the staff and the current residents. "I'm not scared to stop in and say hey," she says. "I'm always welcome there."

25 September 2016

MS. VICKIE, STAFF

Ms. Vickie, a joyful woman with a voice as sweet as sugar, has always had a heart of service. So, when her church, Berean Christian, was looking for an outreach program about five years ago, Ms. Vickie was eager to join them on their expedition. While searching, they came across Gilgal and began a weekly Bible study on Thursdays entitled "Fresh Water-Good News," which the ladies still participate in each week.

Before Ms. Vickie had even stepped through Gilgal's building for the first time, she knew she wanted to be involved with Gilgal, but she didn't expect that she would end up on staff just three years later.

A few years after Berean started their Bible study at Gilgal, Ms. Vickie was in a transitional period with work, always moving from job to job. The ministry head of Berean was aware of Ms. Vickie's search for a steady job, and he approached her one day to tell her that Gilgal had a job opening for a file clerk. Ms. Vickie decided to think about the opportunity wondering if it was what God had planned for her. A few days later, she got her answer. While she was at work, "God said [she] needed to call Ms. Val right now," she says. So, Ms. Vickie picked up the phone, called Ms. Val, and began the process of working at Gilgal. "I just wanted to serve," she says. "I wanted to volunteer and touch the ladies. Me being a part of staff… it's a God thing."

Ms. Vickie is no serving novice. Before she began her job at Gilgal, Ms. Vickie worked in the medical field as a Certified Nursing Assistant, which she now views as God preparing her for her work at Gilgal. In fact, her favorite part about her work at Gilgal is serving and using the gift of encouragement that God has given her.

She also enjoys working with the staff, who she describes as a family. "We support one another, we encourage one another, and because it's a Christ-centered program, we can always talk about God," she says. And as far as working with Ms. Val goes, Ms. Vickie says, "I cannot ask for a better person to work with. I've learned so much as far as how to relate to people, how to give to people, how to love people, how to communicate with people."

Of course, Gilgal would not be Gilgal without the women who fill its doors, and they, too, have been a large part of Ms. Vickie's experience as a staff member. "Interacting with the women…it can be a really good thing," she says, smiling. "Seeing them grow, seeing and watching God do a magnificent thing in their lives…and seeing Him just work out His will in their lives." Ms. Vickie enjoys watching the transformation of the ladies from the inside out, from shy women with low self-esteem to confident, God-fearing women. "It's a wonderful, wonderful thing to see them blossom," she says.

15 August 2016

MELINDA G., CURRENT CLIENT

Melinda G. learned the hard way that drugs don't discriminate. Melinda holds a degree in marketing and for 20 years she worked in IT sales, making a six-figure salary. She and her husband and daughter were living a typical suburban life when she was in a car accident that left her in a lot of pain. The doctor prescribed pain killers, which alleviated the pain, but also brought on an addiction. She knew she was hooked when she missed a doctor's appointment, couldn't get a refill, and went into serious withdrawal. In the meantime, she was pregnant and her daughter was born with severe brain damage. With the stress of caring for a new child and while still on her prescribed pain killers, she didn't see a way to manage everything without being on drugs. One morning, when her second daughter was seven, Melinda went to prepare her breakfast and found her dead. From there, she says, she and her husband "lost it."

Four years later with her home lost and living in her car, she was arrested for Dumpster diving with her husband in Cobb County. "It didn't matter that I had a family," she says. "The pain is so horrific" that she would do anything to make it go away. After her arrest, she spent five months waiting to go to court, detoxing from heroin -- the best alternative she could get to her prescription painkillers -- when she was told by three different people that she needed to complete her rehab at Gilgal. When she was finally able to be seen in court, part of her sentencing was to go to Gilgal. "God got me here," she says.

She's been at Gilgal for 90 days now and she's noticed some changes in herself. "I've already been through the ultimate worse of the worse. I can get through anything," Melinda says. She recognizes that "drugs were a tool to take me away from Christ," she says. She wanted to be in control, but has realized that "God is in full control." She continues "God's plan is to help us prosper." Her walk with Christ has developed too. "I didn't have a relationship with the Lord when I was using," she says. Then she got to the point where she was using so much that "I felt like I had done too much wrong to have a relationship with Christ. I felt like I was irredeemable." But now, she says, she "feel[s] the presence of the Lord on my life. I have hope again that I'm going to be able to be the productive, law-abiding citizen I was before."

For Melinda, being at Gilgal is safe, structured, and peaceful. "It's nice," she says. "I have an opportunity that most people don't get and I feel very blessed. I can put the pieces back together."

18 July 2016

JEANETTE D., VOLUNTEER

Jeanette D. was participating in ministry work at her local Methodist Church one day when a group of women from Gilgal came in. Wanting to know more, a friend put her in touch with Val Cater, director of Gilgal. As Jeanette learned about the organization, she wanted to work with those they served. "It is what it says it is," she says of Gilgal, "a faith-based, Christian facility. It offers a new way to live."

That was four years ago, and now, another ministry that Jeanette helped found, Sobriety Through Affirmation, Reconciliation, Redemption, and Recovery teams up with Gilgal to make referrals, help with counseling, and run workshops for the women. Volunteering with Gilgal gives Jeanette "an opportunity to work with the girls on a direct level and through my ministry with the church," she says.

To be able to give back and to witness the women of Gilgal go through the recovery program and "become beautiful butterflies" gives Jeanette so much joy. The staff and volunteers are "spirit-filled people" who give hope. For Jeanette, the women are able to accomplish what she was able to do when she had no hope.

One of the reasons Jeanette was so attracted to work -- and to continue to work -- with Gilgal is that she too is a recovering addict of almost 20 years. "The Lord led me to them," she says. She "loves those women," and she "knows what they're going through." She says that she knows "what God does in my life. I know that He will transform their lives." Gilgal "gives me an opportunity to give back. Recovery is possible," she says. For her, Gilgal has been both a "benefit and a blessing." It keeps her "humble and keeps [me] level-headed. It reminds me where I came from. She continues, "I see those girls and I see them recovering. I see them getting the support they need. There is no other place like Gilgal."

Jeanette is thankful for the blessing to be able to give back to both her Atlanta community and her community of recovery. "The doors are open" at Gilgal, she says. "They don't care who you are, what you look like, anything about your background other than the fact that you need help. They ask that you come and be serious about it -- with a willing desire." For her, it's not only about the opportunity that led her to Gilgal, though. It's also about the "opportunity the women have to give back and show appreciation for what has been given to them." Gilgal wants their women to be involved in the community. Ms. Val "opens up doors to them...She tries to expose those girls to a lot of things in the community and beyond so that when they get out they have a foundation, a network, contacts. She tries to make sure those girls get exactly what they need so that when they graduate they can stand on their own two feet and have the tools to help them in their recovery." What Ms. Val offers through Gilgal is life, Jeanette says. She offers the women the opportunity to accept it.

28 July 2016

DIANNA K., CURRENT CLIENT

When she was 14, Dianna K. started smoking pot, which led to her trying some pills. Years later she tried coke and meth, and then the last thing she did was crack. "It just took me up -- real fast," she says.

40 years later Dianna stood smoking a cigarette outside one of the Gilgal buildings and felt something gnawing at her. Since she was young she had engaged in illicit substances, but this time was different. Soft spoken and a little timid, she says it was "just kind of a feeling you get inside that you know is not right...you don't feel your peace." Inside, she knew there was something wrong with what she was doing, so she had to tell.

This was a different Dianna than the one 74 days before she lit that cigarette. In her soft, rich Southern accent, she revealed that on her 56th birthday, Dianna had decided that she wanted to make a change in her life. She had been evicted from her home, was homeless, and was addicted to drugs. Her family took her out for a birthday dinner, where they had an intervention. She says she was ready; she was "tired of doing drugs, tired of being homeless, just tired of messing up, so I was ready to change." Her mom was friends with a parishioner at a local church who knew of Gilgal and so referred her here.

Since then, she has been slowly changing everyday. When the ladies first come to Gilgal, she says, "they don't know what to expect and they're kind of laid back, then they start getting into the routine and you start seeing changes." You can tell when someone's going through a transition when their physical features change, Dianna explains. "In their face you see a lightness come over them." For some, their posture becomes more erect, less hunched. For others, their faces clear up from skin problems and they begin to smile.

But these changes come slowly, through daily scripture readings, reflections, and prayer. Every morning Dianna is up with her housemates at 6:30 to read and discuss Proverbs. From there, the women read Our Daily Bread and reflect on their scripture devotionals. They pray, eat breakfast, and complete their chores before beginning their morning classes.

She has started seeing changes in herself too. The hardship that came as a result of her addiction doesn't burden her as much anymore.

Slowly she's started to feel her shoulders lighten too. She can tell that "the Holy Spirit's inside me right now." If she does something that makes her feel uneasy and not at peace with herself, He convicts her to make the change. She sees it with her decision to quit doing drugs, to quit smoking, to turn herself in for smoking at Gilgal, so that she can find the success she has neglected for so long. Success for her, Dianna says, is "to be able to have enough money to pay your bills and not have to worry about it, not have to worry about drugs all the time or where you're going to get your next meal or how you're going to pay your bills. And just be happy. Have peace of mind. And know I'll never do drugs again."

8 June 2016

MS. PHYLLIS., GRADUATE

When clients, volunteers, and visitors alike walk into Gilgal, a warm smile greets them. This is the face of Ms. Phyllis, long-time volunteer and first Gilgal graduate. When I interviewed Ms. Phyllis, she was wearing a purple smock that brought out the richness of her caramel skin. Her short hair was pulled into a high and tight ponytail, and she spoke excitedly with her ringed hands and braceleted wrists. She was ready to share her life story, the undulations of her voice rising and falling with the twists and turns of her experiences -- from memories that brought her joy to those she revealed in a whisper. We traveled from Miami to Gainesville to Jacksonville to Atlanta, following the circuitous path of her life and her memories.

Ms. Phyllis' story begins as a young child growing up in Miami. She began experimenting with drugs and by the time she was 12 she was selling Quaaludes. After she graduated from high school she started running with a crowd who was shooting up heroin and Demerol. Her voice breaks from her storytelling into a whisper: "All of them are dead now except one person and me." Within a year, she continues, she met the man who would father her two children. This same man was partially responsible for the loss of four fingers on her right hand. They were mainlining drugs one night and the drugs went directly into her artery, cutting off the blood supply from her wrist to her hand. Because they were then high, they didn't consider going immediately to the hospital. But eventually the went. They amputated her fingers and she spent three months recovering. During this time, she stewed over the what her husband had done: inserte the IV right into her artery. Forgiveness and responsibility were only to come later.

Ms. Phyllis' extended stay at the hospital following her amputatio afforded her the opportunity to begin her first try with rehabilitation for her drug addiction. She enrolled in a 30-day program and within five yea believed she had "gotten her life back." Within a year she was remarried, was in technical school, and received a position as a paid intern. This allowed her time to get back on her feet, because soon she again found her self in trouble. So she moved to Jacksonville, Florida and started workin as a food service employee in a hospital. They provided job training and she was steady again. But it wouldn't last for long. She started to sense

90

that there was an imbalance in her -- her head would spin and she would get headaches. Around this time her second husband proved to be no less abusive than the first. Seeing a way out, she fled to Atlanta.

She was aimless for a bit and was living in motels, but eventually ended up in a men's homeless shelter. About to give up and with nowhere to turn, the pastor of the center came to talk to her and hear her story. Soon he had gotten her a room in a women's shelter in Dahlonega. She would come to spend two and a half years there, eventually becoming head cook for 28 women, a feat she first thought was impossible. She would become the assistant house manager when the head house manager went to look for a job at Gilgal. Ms. Val hired the house manager and ended up moving all the women from the house in Dahlonega to Atlanta. While her house manager drove the moving truck, Ms. Phyllis rode in the car with Ms. Val and they got to talking. By the time they had completed the drive from the mountains, Ms. Phyllis was looking forward to her new home and potential new full sobriety as a client at Gilgal.

A large part of Gilgal's method to help their clients achieve life-long sobriety is getting to the root cause of why women begin their addictions in the first place. By the time Ms. Phyllis reached Gilgal, she had been largely ignoring these root causes. She knew that something was wrong -- the headaches and spinning that had plagued her in Jacksonville had followed her to Atlanta -- and she turned to God to stabilize her. She sought prayer because she saw her grandmother pray, but for her, it was more about tradition than developing a personal relationship with God. At Gilgal she discovered that she had learned how to help family members when they were in trouble, but not others; she learned that she had some trouble with prejudices. Gilgal helped her to dismantle these narrow visions of others and what it meant to love.

She says, "When I came I was so overwhelmed by someone opening their doors for someone who they had never even met before." She continues, "I didn't have anywhere to lay my head...for someone to open their house up to me without no pay, feed me, shelter me, all because they want to know how they can be of service to women of our status" transformed her. She was able to see "the manifestation of God." No longer was God simply the tradition of prayer. Now, "He had a personality. He could do the impossible. I began to believe in God." From here, she "had a heart-changing." She knew what she needed to do.

Ms. Phyllis was able to admit to her drug addiction and the anger she harbored against her first husband and daughter. She knew she had to confess to her anger and her pain. She realized, "I have purpose, I have heart, in the way we're supposed to treat one another." She continues, "I was committed to just my family...But could I really show you love?" It was at Gilgal where she learned to show true compassion and giving her heart not just because she was doing "servant work" and was supposed to, but because she truly loves God and therefore loves His people. She learned to be obedient to God now, and not to the limitations of man.

Since she graduated 10 years ago, Ms. Phyllis has been working and volunteering at Gilgal. Sometimes it's hard -- she says that "in the personalities of each woman you can see in every one of them a part of you." But despite this, "miracles happen," Ms. Phyllis intones, with the same seriousness reserved for the most harrowing parts of her story. She likes being surrounded by "Ms. Val and the circle of strong women." Her strength is nurturing. She continues, "if I could say to someone something that will help ease their pain, their hurt, or something they can learn that will help them be better on their journey, then that's what I love doing. We all come from different walks of life, but we are all God's children."

4 August 2016

LASHUN R., GRADUATE

Father,

Thank you for another day of revelation, revealing your Power that lives within me, Your Holy Spirit is all I need to stay on the path of righteousness, you said, Just Trust Thee.

Lord, You whisper to me and told me my feelings were out to hurt me. You told me don't get involved with what I feel, just tap into the Truth and stand still. The feelings You have so blessed me with are only feelings, they don't last forever but Your love for me do. Continue to follow Me into All Truth, what I say is real my child, so you got to keep it real too. I'm always here right by your side to help you, if you just let me take control as I shape and mold you. I have a purpose I created you for. You were chosen don't you know you belong to me? I knew you would come when I called your name Lashun bringing glory unto me. You must not look to man to make you feel good, keep your eyes on Me and I will take care of you, love you, comfort you, embrace you, caress you, protect you, walk with you, talk to you, keep you, carry you, and I will make love to you too. I am God, you can do all things through Christ who strengthens you I'm always the same, my word never changes. Don't look back Lashun, claim Victory over all things. I have All Power and I will never let you down, I'm giving you a gift, where is your faith Lashun? Remember once you were lost but now you are found. My Son name Jesus came to your rescue, and die on the cross for you, that's because I'm your Father in Heaven, I love you no matter what, My love for you is always and forever. So you must stay in my will don't give up Lashun on what you just feel. I got you in the palm of my hands, we will be together for eternity- Heaven The Promise Land.

Yes, Lord, I give You all the praise, honor and glory worshipping you thank you for revelation, revealing the truth. It is in Your precious son named Jesus, I Love You Too. To God Be the Glory Amen, Amen Thank You Jesus for Saving My Life.

A conversation with God written by Lashun R.

2009

XYLINA I., CURRENT CLIENT

Xylina means "of the woods" in Greek. Yet she grew up in the desert. Her mother was supposed to care for her. Yet started her on drugs and kept her that way until three years ago when Xylina "split from her." The law declares her an adult, and in many ways she is an old soul who knows more and has seen more than her age reveals. Yet she seeks to reclaim her lost childhood through her drawings and animations.

Xylina found Gilgal two months ago after a failed suicide attempt. In fact, she was about to throw herself in front of a car, but instead the driver of the car pulled over, took her out to dinner, and brought her to the hospital. There, she was given a list of programs to call and at random chose Gilgal. Someone on the other end picked up right away. "By the grace of God I am here," she says.

Being at Gilgal has "opened up my world view of everything," says Xylina. Her first 30 days were a rough transition where she realized she was an addict. She came to understand that her "thought patterns weren't normal thought patterns. I could just think of my addictions," she says. But in the last two months, her world has been totally thrown upside down: she didn't "know my left from my right, my up from my down," she says.

Her troubles began when she was five when her mom started constantly drugging her. She believes "my mom was ill of some sort." She would drug Xylina with a psychotic, which created hallucinations and a sense of paranoia. By the time she was eight she was completely paranoic and believed that someone was coming to get her. By the time she was 19 she "wanted to get away from the drug-induced haze" and called her aunt and uncle for help. She was told that she had an hour to pack her things and get on a flight to Atlanta, where she would live with her aunt and uncle. It was in Atlanta that she discovered that she was a moderately functioning alcoholic, but it was getting harder and harder to hold a job and to find a stable place to live. Soon she was seeking drugs just to get high. "Last year," she says, "I was non-stop, completely drunk for the whole year." Eventually her uncle kicked her out and part of her was not sure why. In her family, "it was acceptable to be high, drunk, whatever."

Life at Gilgal has played out in sharp relief to her days in the des-

ert. She says, "there's no abuse, no neglect. It's truly amazing here." She laughs and continues, "it is a house full of women, but it's like I'm living with a whole bunch of sisters, my family." In her two months she's seen a lot of growth and maturity in herself and in her sisters. For her, she says, "it's tough. I'm starting to identify my feelings more. Trying to maintain and deal with my feelings more. Sometimes I'll get angry for no reason -- from bottling stuff up, or from a flashback -- and learning to deal with it in the right way is challenging. It's like I'm reborn again. Learning to deal with it in a new way."

Gilgal is the safest place Xylina has ever been. She thought she would be dead before she was 20 if she stayed with her mom, constantly looking at death and despair in her drug-induced haze. But here, at Gilgal, "is a whole new world. This is the best place I've ever been," she says. "I've never experienced the love the staff here has for every person who walks through these doors. It's truly amazing." She has learned that God is here in the "genuineness of the place. I am really getting to know Him. Even if you're broken, they'll help fix you -- even just from the love alone. The love here is amazing," she says. When Xylina arrived at Gilgal's doors, Ms. Val said to her, "Welcome and I love you so much. She opened this program, has taken us all in, and she doesn't even know any of us. She's truly an angel," says Xylina.

Her favorite moment at Gilgal is when "the good pastors" come in. She says, "I love hearing the Word and knowing that it does get better and it will get better."

2 August 2016

CALLIE R., GRADUATE

Callie R. has a thick Southern accent that drips of honey. She laughs easily and smiles as she reminisces about who she was before Gilgal, chuckling and shaking her head at the person who made choices that were not always in her best interest. But all that changed when she encountered Gilgal.

Callie grew up in a house where many of the people in it suffered from addiction. She says this past was "broken," but that it was normal for her. Raised by her aunt, she still had contact with her birth mother and was "raised around my mom's addiction, raised around her stomach getting pumped, raised around seeing her behind prison glass." This was life, and by the time she was 13, things started to get really bad. First her aunt and grandfather passed away on the same day. Her grandmother soon broke her hip and went to live with her addict grandson. By the time she was 16 the responsibility fell fully on Callie to take care of her grandmother. In the same year, her mother and brother were in a horrific car accident and her brother passed away as a result of the injuries he sustained. This was what broke the dam. To help her deal with her pain, anger, and hurt, her older brother gave her her first beer and showed her how to cut her arms. She was angry at God and wanted to get away from all that was happening. "I was basically just lost," she says about this time in her life.

Within a year, the pills that she had fastidiously avoided because she saw what they had done to her birth mother was what she craved. She had money, so she could get the pills and drugs that she wanted. Looking back on it now, Callie says, "I was looking for love and didn't know where to find it."

Despite her vulnerabilities, Callie put on a strong face. She turned to music to help drown out her thoughts. "I thought I was Superwoman," she says. "But I was lost."

The year Callie turned 19 marked another turning point. Her mother, having taken too many pills, overdosed. Callie knew something was wrong, but she was high too and her cousins, who were also high, wouldn't let her call for help. Callie was finally able to call some friends

who placed her mom face down on the bottom bunk of a bunk bed. Her last words were, "I'm trying." Later that night her mom passed away, while Callie was high and passed out in the top bunk. "Broken hands were raising a broken child," she says.

She soon descended into a deep depression and thoughts of suicide haunted her. To cope, she began heavily cutting, drinking, taking pills, and getting into destructive relationships. "Beer was my bread," she says. "And I caused destruction all around me. I didn't want to exist. I felt like I was a burden. I didn't feel loved anymore. I felt like I deserved Hell and I wanted to die. I was very angry with God and I just didn't care anymore." In the pit of despair, Callie looked for the sharpest knife in the house. Unable to find one, she took what she could find and started to cut away at her wrists. Her aunt, who raised her, discovered what she had done, and Callie ran out to the woods behind her house. As she heard the sirens of the emergency vehicles get closer, she recalls, "I could run. Or I could surrender."

She was committed to a mental hospital and, laying there, realized that she "had a choice. I could be like the rest of my family -- I had seen what addiction had done firsthand" -- but she decided she didn't want that anymore. She received a list of rehabilitation facilities to call, and she went down the list contacting them. On her second call, she says, "the sweetest voice picked up the phone. It was the voice of Ms. Val Cater."

Ms. Val told her what she needed to do, and she was admitted into Gilgal.

For Callie, the first 30 days were the hardest. She had never been away from her mom for an extended period of time and she thought that the goal was merely to stabilize her drinking habits so she could "go back and get drunk with my sisters. I thought people here were crazy," she recalls. "Out their dang mind! People were telling me to make my bed, women were telling me to quit cussing." But she didn't have anywhere else to go: "my mother had told Gilgal that I couldn't come home."

Despite the difficulty of those first 30 days, "God began dealing with me immediately in my heart," Callie says. "He began to deal with me on the anger I had towards Him with losing my brother and my birth mother." For Callie, "the Holy Spirit became such a powerful intimate presence. And not just on my soul, but the souls of everyone here." Callie thrived -- although not easily -- on the structure of Gilgal. She says, "My Mama tried to 'discipline' me as best she could. But she wasn't able to train me up in a Godly structure. At Gilgal, I was able to be trained up in the Lord."

"I had a lot of anger," Callie continues. "I had a struggle with anger. I had a lot of hurt. But Gilgal was equipped with the soldiers and generals of Christ to be able to to handle that. For me, I needed to be fought with, I needed to be loved, I needed to be counseled." Journaling began to have a life-changing impact on Callie's life and soon she found herself committing to Gilgal and staying. "Going back is not an option," Callie says. "Relapse was not an option. This is where I met Jesus," Callie continues. "This is where I was loved on. Given tools. Given patience. I met so many beautiful people in the Lord. I didn't even know people like this existed. They are the hands and feet of Jesus." Callie becomes very serious. "So many of us have been tossed aside, told we were nothing. Been treated like a piece of property." But at Gilgal, she saw "how much love and how God works through people -- the volunteers and the staff."

"But it wasn't always good," Callie says. "I had 11 write ups. I almost got kicked out three times. But they had patience. It's the love and the patience of Jesus Christ." Callie had a breakthrough when "the Holy Spirit revealed to me that empty place inside of me. The root issue behind me looking for love in the women and the men. He healed that place and delivered me. This is where I met Jesus," Callie continues, "the lover of my soul. To know that He is my very breath and existence. He is my strength when I can't even walk. Hallelujah I met His presence."

Having graduated from Gilgal, Callie is now pursuing her bachelor's degree in early childhood education. "I was running like Jonah," Callie says, and she asked God for a sign, and there was a billboard on the side of the highway that said, "become a teacher."

When asked how she maintains her faith and sobriety in the difficulties of the world, Callie says, you "gotta keep your head up. The Word will sustain you. And God is the Word. He has called me and is using me to be the Joseph of my family -- to call others out of darkness."

Callie is a woman transformed. Superwoman indeed.

7 June 2016

EPILOGUE

Where are they now? Updates on the "Current Clients" of Gilgal.

Shelly F: Graduated August 5, 2016
Xylina I: Continuing with Gilgal
Dianna K: Left the program
Samantha P: Left the program
Melinda G: Continuing with Gilgal
Magen G: Left the program
Yulondor F: Continuing with Phase II of Gilgal
Tammy M: Continuing with Gilgal
Kristi Q: Continuing with Phase II of Gilgal

As you conclude your reading of the "Stories of Gilgal," we want to remind you that these stories represent only a fraction of Gilgal Inc. With any recovery program, there will be the clients who don't make it to graduation day, but that does not mean their story ends when they choose to or are asked to leave.

When I returned to Gilgal to start giving piano lessons in January of 2014, Ms. Val informed us that the woman who had requested the piano lessons had decided to leave the program. Yet, three years later, my life has been changed and still continues to be changed because of her. Each time one walks through Gilgal's doors, a seed is planted and grows inevitably, reaching people in many different ways and forms. The woman wh asked for lessons may not have, but the seed Gilgal planted within her brought on an unavoidable change in me that I hope to plant in someone else.

-Catherine J. and Naitnaphit L.

Made in the USA
San Bernardino, CA
09 November 2016